T0328341

Before Literature

Before Literature examines storytelling that, whether due to historical, technological, or socio-economic circumstance, is neither shaped nor influenced by alphabetic literacy.

How does a story unfold when carried solely in memory, when it cannot be written down or externally stored? What structural and stylistic pressures are imposed when it must travel through space and time exclusively by word of mouth? In *Before Literature*, Sheila J. Nayar addresses these very questions, guiding the reader in a lively and accessible manner through the key features of storytelling that's been unaffected by writing. Even more, Nayar shows how the very norms that drove oral epics such as the *Mahabharata* and Homer's *Odyssey* can continue to shape contemporary forms like Bollywood masala films, Hollywood spectaculars, and comic books.

This clear and accessible guide is an ideal starting point for undergraduates approaching the study of orality. It offers a fundamentally different way of thinking about oral narrative, while also disclosing some of the "hows" and "whys" of written literature, leading to a much broader understanding and appreciation of our storytelling tradition.

Sheila J. Nayar is Professor of English, Communication and Media Studies at Greensboro College, North Carolina, USA.

Before Literature

The Nature of Narrative Without the Written Word

Sheila J. Nayar

Routledge
Taylor & Francis Group

LONDON AND NEW YORK

First published 2020
by Routledge
4 Park Square, Milton Park, Abingdon, Oxon OX14 4RN

and by Routledge
605 Third Avenue, New York, NY 10017

Routledge is an imprint of the Taylor & Francis Group, an informa business

British Library Cataloguing-in-Publication Data
A catalogue record for this book is available from the British Library

Library of Congress Cataloging-in-Publication Data
A catalog record has been requested for this book

ISBN: 978-0-367-24281-7 (hbk)
ISBN: 978-0-367-24280-0 (pbk)
ISBN: 978-0-429-28154-9 (ebk)

Typeset in Bembo
by Newgen Publishing UK

To Shardha, Rohan, Sangeeta, Shaan, and Anika

Contents

Figures

Acknowledgments

The names of many of those to whom I owe scholarly grati-
tude appear throughout this book. Still, one among them, Walter
J. Ong, deserves additional acknowledgment for having been
willing many years ago, notwithstanding his being in his 80s, to
communicate with a nascent film scholar who had somehow
unexpectedly wandered into the field of orality-literacy studies.
Others whose impact has been no less intellectually significant
include my mother Nancy Ann Nayar, for (just as unexpectedly)
spawning that wandering. It was she, after all, who recommended
that I might find Ong's *Orality and Literacy* an interesting read.
(Who could have guessed where it would lead?) Others to
whom I am indebted include my husband Thomas W. Shields,
who participated in virtually all the positing and percolations that
have gone into the multiple manifestations of this material. My
father Baldev Raj Nayar has been unflagging in his support and
his commitment to keeping me on my research heels, notwithstanding that he himself is now in his 80s. I owe much to media
ecologist Lance Strate, who was instrumental in shepherding my
earliest orality-literacy expedition into the book world, much
as Paul Soukup has assisted me in sustaining its life thereafter.
Colleagues and friends who have served as ears, eyes, guides,
and more include Kathleen Keating, Wayne Johns, Jane Girardi,
Charles Hebert, George Cheatham, Judy Cheatham, Michelle
Plaisance, Paul Leslie, Jean Shields, and Anna Reisman. I am
grateful, too, to Polly Dodson and Routledge for deciding that

this was a book worth publishing, as well as to several generations of students, as it was they whom I initially had in mind when embarking on this project. And while officially I have dedicated this book to my nieces and nephews who symbolically comprise for me the next generation of readers, I wish unofficially to dedicate *Before Literature* to those who won't be reading this book—simply and unfortunately because skills-wise they can't. Indeed, my hope is that, in being exposed to just how much literacy matters, readers of this book will be spurred to assist—or, at the least, be more sensitive to—those who have been denied the privileges that reading and writing foster.

1 Denaturalizing literacy

Does a fish know that it lives in water? Even more, does it know that it lives its entire life wet? You're probably thinking: Well, certainly a fish would register something bodily about its natural environment were it reeled out of the ocean and tossed onto a dry, sunbaked pier.

So, let's imagine this exiled fish were a thinking animal, voluntarily able to form thoughts and judgments. Once extracted from the water, so much it didn't know about that environment would suddenly become all too painfully apparent. The agony would be there in its registered incapacity to breathe or swim away to safety, and in its skin drying out in the aridity of the air and the heat of the sun. And, of course, the only thing that fish would want would be to get *back* into that environment it had never before experienced *as* an environment—the water it gulped, the wetness that kept its scales from withering.

If you are reading this, then you are that fish, and this book, *Before Literature*, is the tackle and pier. This is a book intent on wresting you out of an environment that has become so natural for you, so *naturalized*, that you—me—we—are hardly even aware of how artificial, constructed, and unnatural it is. What I'm talking about here could go by several names: reading, writing, literacy, inscription, the alphabet. Even more, these have aided and productively invaded human culture for so long that other names now travel alongside them: cuneiform, papyri, scrolls, manuscripts, vellum, paper, the printing press, libraries, encyclopedias, atlases, journals, novels, textbooks, pulp fiction, the manual for your dishwasher, street signs, digital media, bestsellers about American history, even *history* as a concept and field of study—in fact, pretty much all fields of study, including science, economics, and literature certainly, but also finance, biology, political science—which means pretty much everything done in the educational setting. So, while literacy is by no means a force to condemn, we do need to be aware that it is cultural, not natural. No child is born knowing how to read and write—although, without developing a mastery of letters these days, said child might well get left behind in life. Think of this book, then, the way a medical student might her premed courses: as what you ought to know before embarking on any study of literature; as a kind of indispensable *prelit*, as it were.

But, first, some necessary qualifications: Although I will be using the word *reading* foremost in the context of alphabetically derived literacy, reading as an activity and skill has been around far longer than any script that represents sounds (phonemes) through symbols. Thought expressed in material symbols—or graphism, as it's sometimes called—existed for millennia before the development of the phonetic alphabet, in such forms as totem carvings, pictographs, petroglyphs, nicks on branches, and even designs in textiles. True, these might have facilitated a singer's recall of a narrative, but they did not in and of themselves carry a narrative wholesale. Also, while my emphasis on alphabetic literacy may appear to jettison cultures that use logographic systems of writing (where a single character can represent an entire word or phrase, as in Chinese), often I use the term more as a shorthand—as way of differentiating this book's focus, which is *writing*-based literacy (and, so, potentially inclusive of the logographic), from other forms of literacy such as "media literacy" or "visual literacy."

So, back now to the theme of reading as an unnatural phenomenon: Keep in mind that, by the time the average student graduates from college, they have spent almost two decades (20 years!) being initiated, instructed, and, yes, even indoctrinated into a literate mindset; into accepting that reading and writing are such vital, mandatory skills that one cannot be a full-fledged citizen without them—that one perhaps isn't even fully human without them. This schooling entails learning not only *to* read (the alphabet, storybooks, textbooks, and so on), but also *how* to read and, so, unavoidably, too, how to think. As Stanislas Dehaene, neuroscientist and author of *Reading in the Brain*, explains, "the acquisition of reading entails massive functional changes in children's brains."[1] But because as readers we have been so *overtrained*—the word is his—we can hardly evaluate any longer how difficult the act of reading truly is. We can, however, glean something about the complexity of the process just by looking at what parts of the brain get activated depending on whether we are vocalizing or visualizing language (only the literate mindset is capable of doing the latter). [1]

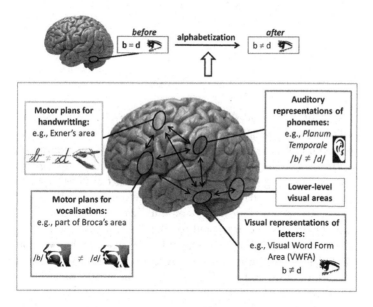

Figure 1.1 Brain areas involved in literacy acquisition. Cutting-edge research today in neuroscience is proving that the acquisition of literacy literally reorganizes the human brain. (Image courtesy of F. Pegado, K. Nakamura, and T. Hannagan [2014] "How Does Literacy Break Mirror Invariance in the Visual System?" *Frontiers in Psychology* 5:703 /Creative Commons by 3.0.)

Note: It is also true, as Maryanne Wolf reminds us, that "[e]ach writing system requires something a little different in how the brain organizes itself to read ..." (*Tales of Literacy*, 34).

If extricating oneself neurologically from one's history of reading seems challenging, no less arduous is trying not to *think* like a reader. It's a bit like trying to force someone into forgetting how to ride a bicycle or into un-reading the last sentence they just read. In fact, as a brisk way experiencing how difficult disentangling yourself from yourself as a reading individual is, try this: Get online and google "Stroop Test." Take the test, which asks you to identify the color of several given words, and see how well you are able to fare. For those not in reach of a computer, here's a modified version in black and white:

Name the color of the ink in these words:

black

white

gray

Did your brain read the words first in lieu of identifying their colors? We are hardly aware of the extent to which our alphabetic environment has cognitively molded us until we are confronted with an exercise like this. Our system of understanding, our way of knowing—our epistemic state (from the Greek *epistêmê* for knowledge)—has become like that water in which the fish exists. We become less and less mindful that we live and function (and breathe) in a constructed paradigm. If you can't fathom life without mobile phones or the Internet, imagine life without inscription—which is, of course, what gave rise to both cellular communication and the Web, including the latter's binary code based on 0 and 1.

This is precisely the environment from which *Before Literature* plans to liberate you—or to straitjacket you, alternatively, into a prelit way of knowing. This book will take away not only your Internet and mobile phones, conceptually speaking, but also everything and anything that has to do with narrative when shaped fundamentally by inscription. In a sense, you'll be placed in the physical and cognitive circumstance upon which Vladimir

Nabokov ruminated in his novel *Pale Fire*: "What if we awake one day, all of us, and find ourselves utterly unable to read?"[2] The focus here, consequently, will be on epics and myths, folktales and fairy tales (and even movies and novels) that bear signs of having been molded by a way of knowing that came before (or that, in some cases, desirably avoids) alphabetic literacy. That's why this book's title signals narrative *before* literature. The very word "literature" derives from the Latin *littera* or *litera*, meaning "alphabetic letter." Literature, in other words—at least at the strictest etymological level—is a body of *written* works. Or, as Robert Scholes and Robert Kellogg more forcefully pronounce in *The Nature of Narrative*, literature "is by definition the art of letters."[3] And when storytelling can be generated in writing—which is to say, with the use of such technologies as quill, pencil, printing press, code—it can achieve far more plasticity than when forced to rely exclusively on what philosopher and cognitive scientist Andy Clark shrewdly calls our "naked brain."[4]

But back to those stories that were passed down before or without the technology of writing—which is to say, by way of our acoustical senses alone. See, before we became literate—not only individually but also as a society—we were all of us *oral*. Our narratives, our stories, our collective history before the discipline of history, traveled by way of memory, which itself traveled almost exclusively from one person's tongue to another's ear. What's more, this transmission had to happen through successive generations, sometimes for centuries. Henri-Jean Martin offers a handy analogy in *The History of Power of Writing*. If writing goes back 5,000 years in the annals of humanity, only the last page of those annals would comprise the entire age of *Homo scribens*, or writing man. As for the print era ushered in by Johannes Gutenberg—that would correspond to a mere five lines. And our contemporary mass media? Those "would appear only in the last line, with telecommunications occupying no more space than a final '?'."[5]

Keep in mind, too, that narratives operating out of an oral way of knowing didn't simply disappear with the rise of *Homo scribens*. As we shall see, we can find them all around us still.

And yet, many in the field of literature have decided that foregrounding an oral way of knowing—sometimes even acknowledging its possibility—is taboo. One current scholar even referred to the pioneering works published in the field in the 1960s as constituting "social-science fictions."[6] The intimation was that those who had first studied and developed a critical awareness of orality's relationship to communication and the history of the book had presented their work in the guise of ethnography. Suffice it to say that my own research, compounded by some personal history that I'll reveal in the next chapter, lands me squarely in the camp of those pioneers. (I'll be calling on one of them shortly, in fact.)

But why this recent, and sometimes unsympathetic, turn in literary studies away from recognizing the potential sway of orality? Is it because, like that fish in the water, we're oblivious to our own alphabetically literate paradigm? Or, do we choose to turn our heads because acknowledging that paradigm might unsettle or too acutely expose the extent of our privilege? After all, there are plenty of people even today who can neither read nor write, or who have not been sufficiently trained to do so in a way that makes them proficiently literate. Perhaps, then, maintaining that a culture is oral, or that certain populations might prefer oral ways of knowing, is interpreted as signifying *illiteracy*—with the very word "oral" therefore construed as something inherently demeaning, an insult. So, rather than acknowledge this mentality or episteme in a nondisparaging manner, some folks prefer simply to deny it. But as philosopher Dan Dennett has insisted (here channeled through the words of reading scholar Maryanne Wolf) "*what went before* is evolutionarily important to understand"[7]— and in no small measure, I need add, because that *before* is *still going on*.

Notes

1   Dehaene, *Reading in the Brain*, 218.
2   Nabokov, *Pale Fire*, 289.
3   Scholes and Kellogg, *Nature of Narrative*, 17.

4 Clark, *Mindware*, 153.
5 Martin, *History and Power*, 1.
6 Price, "Introduction," 9.
7 Wolf, *Tales of Literacy*, 77.

References

Clark, Andy. *Mindware: An Introduction to the Philosophy of Cognitive Science*. New York: Oxford University Press, 2001.

Dehaene, Stanislas. *Reading in the Brain: The New Science of How We Read*. New York: Penguin Books, 2010.

Martin, Henri-Jean. *The History and Power of Writing*. Trans. Lydia G. Cochrane. Chicago: University of Chicago Press, 1994.

Nabokov, Vladimir. *Pale Fire*. New York: Vintage International, 1989.

Price, Leah. "Introduction: Reading Matter." *PMLA* 121, 1 (January 2006): 9–16.

Scholes, Robert, and Robert Kellogg. *The Nature of Narrative*. Oxford: Oxford University Press, 1968.

Wolf, Maryanne. *Tales of Literacy for the 21st Century*. Oxford: Oxford University Press, 2016.

2 The story behind *Before Literature*

There's a swift way to dismantle any notion that the oral episteme is somehow the offensive signal of a "lesser" way of knowing. But before we get there, I first want to tell you my story: how it was that I came to learn of the power, import, and particularities of narrative shaped by *orality*—a word, incidentally, that Microsoft Word's spellcheck neither acknowledges nor even recognizes as genuine. It's also a story that highlights how academic scholarship can sometimes be informed by personal experience, not to mention, a modicum of luck when it comes to timing.

Back in the 1990s, I embarked on a project perhaps best described as a kind of visual anthropology. It was, to be sure, an entirely un-literary endeavor, such that I would procure no status by aligning myself with the likes of Shakespeare, or Jane Austen, or even modernist art films. Nope, I was going to analyze the superhit films produced by Bollywood, the Hollywood of Bombay (now Mumbai), especially those that ranged from the 1970s to the 1990s. Academics at the time—but, even more, educated Indians—would often ask with a kind of flummoxed expression what possibly I thought I was going to learn. As it turned out, a lot. While today's Hindi-film blockbusters can still sometimes display the characteristics of the older movies—a love for musical numbers, say, an appreciation of spectacle—20th-century Bollywood was a very different place. The latter half of that century saw the zenith of the masala or spice-mix film. Masala films were basically formula films: "all singing, all dancing, all fighting," as the popular adage went. Each offered not only musical numbers and martial arts, but also dollops of romance, melodrama, and comedy skits. The films were excessive and spectacular—notwithstanding that far more of them failed than succeeded at the box office. (Bollywood even has a category for the former sort: superflops.) By the 1970s, movies were being churned out in startling numbers, often with shoddy production values that sadly matched the oft-shoddy nature of the theaters in which they were screened. In part, this was because India's elite audiences were now retreating for the purposes of entertainment to the domestic arena—which is to say, into their sitting rooms around their new TVs.

Spurred by the fact that I myself was half-Indian, half-Anglo-American, I decided to focus on films that had been adapted from Hollywood. And there were many: versions of classics such as *Sabrina* and *On the Waterfront*, as well as more contemporaneous films, such as *Indecent Proposal, A Kiss Before Dying,* and *What About Bob?* My intention was to tease out what changes were repeatedly made to the Hollywood films in order to render their storylines culturally indigenous and palatable to India's domestic audiences. Because I restricted myself exclusively to films that had been highly successful with audiences—recall that this was a landscape littered with superflops—I was, unbeknownst to me at the time, internalizing the storytelling norms that these movies virtually always shared. By "norms" I mean not only what the films revealed or projected regarding cultural values, such as having to do with love, marriage, heroism, religion, familial relations, sex, and so on; but also what patterns tended to undergird the films' content, style, and form. For instance, what secondary storylines had to be added? Was the original story compressed or strung out? How was the dialogue different, not only in terms of substance but delivery? What variations were there in editing, camera movement, framing, even special effects? Were the sets and costumes more elaborate or less? Was the filmic palette more colorful or more muted?

Like I said, at the time, I was cataloguing these recurrent patterns and themes as evidence of what made the films culturally

Figure 2.1 Bollywood movie poster for the mid-1970s blockbuster *Deewar* (lit. The Wall, dir. Salim-Javed, 1975), starring Amitabh Bhachchan. Courtesy of Alamy. *Deewar* tells the story of two brothers raised in impoverished circumstances who end up on opposite sides of the law—one becomes a policeman, the other a criminal. Superstar Bachchan plays the delinquent "angry you man," a character putatively modeled on an actual Bombay gangster. The film's theme of vigilante crime and its kinetic exhibition of martial arts are supplemented, like all films of the period, with a half-dozen musical numbers.

relevant and resonant. As housed in box-office hits, these were the features, or so I thought, that were rendering the films distinctly Indian—at least for those largely working-class, theater-going spectators. So, it came as a startling surprise when an offhanded book recommendation by my mother, who also happens to be a Sanskrit scholar (and the Anglo-American parent), sent me reeling—straight into an intellectual paradigm shift. In fact, this book she recommended, merely because she thought I might find it "interesting," would completely alter the course of my scholarly career.

The book was *Orality and Literacy*,[1] by Walter J. Ong, a Jesuit literary scholar—and one of those explicitly called out for having produced a social-science fiction. But, to me, what Ong was saying did not feel at all like sociological invention, given that I had experienced something, even if only by chance, that many Western academics likely hadn't: a long-term engagement with an individual who was comfortably nonliterate—which is to say, who existed in a culture where her orality was not something inherently shameful or in need of concealing; where societal allowances had in fact been made for people who could not read, let alone write. In other words, when I read Ong's book and for the first time was acquainted with the concept of orality, I could see nothing fictitious about what he was arguing because it was *all so familiar*—and on two entirely different fronts. (And so, yes, in nerd-like fashion, I read that very nonfictional book in a single sitting, as if it were a nail-biting thriller like Dan Brown's *The Da Vinci Code* or a volume from the Harry Potter series.)

The first of these fronts related to Bollywood: So many of the norms of orality, which Ong had synthetically collated from the works of a range of scholars, including anthropologists, social psychologists, linguists, classicists, scholars of literature, and more, were the very ones on which decades of superhit masala films had hinged. While this may surprise some readers, given that film is an entirely modern medium, in certain ways that importation maked logical sense. While today India's literacy rate has soared to above 74 percent, at the time of India's independence from colonial British rule in 1947—when the Bombay film formula first began to take shape—it was a mere 12 percent. By the 1970s, it had reached approximately 34 percent, and 52 percent by 1991. On a broader scale, by 1980, the world literacy rate was approximately 56 percent, having risen from 21 percent in 1900. So, it seems only fitting that individuals denied literacy in the twentieth century might have inadvertently shaped segments of popular visual media according to oral principles of narrative. What better way for spectators un-steeped in reading to engage with, and even unwittingly mold, narrative than in a movie theater? (Certainly they could not rely on the ancient oral epics as now printed on the page!)

In other words—and as we shall address more concretely in the coming chapters—a narrative fashioned on the basis of an oral way of knowing, whether consciously or not, is very different from one that engages with orality as a theme. Compare this difference, if you will, to a book written *for* a blind child (with its text in Braille) to one *about* experiencing that state, as in a novel like José Saramago's *Blindness*. While some readers may cringe at my association of the 1970s–1990s masala film with orality, I see nothing odious or demeaning about that connection. What, after all, is discriminatory about a form of entertainment that gave millions of spectators who could not engage with print—and, so, who were often of the subsidiary or subaltern classes—an access to stories?

But, as I intimated earlier, the possibility of those films serving as evidence of an "oral episteme of visual narrative" was certified by another front, this one not only personal, but outright familial: my own grandmother. This was my paternal grandmother, who had been born and raised in a village in the Gujrat district of the Punjab at a time when its girls did not regularly attend school. As a result, she had never learned to read or write. In fact, so crucial was my grandmother to vitalizing orality for me as a lived experience—as distinct from (as it can only be for some scholars) a mere theoretical abstraction—that it merits my pausing here to quote at length the opening of my very first publication on the topic. For there I describe how, while my grandmother, Jaswant Kaur Nayar, continuously urged her grandchildren to engage in the tasks of the literate ("*Parho, pharo*" was her frequent injunction, "Read, read."), she herself did not. She owned only one book, which consisted of a single word, "Rama," repeated over and over, for several dozen pages. I remember as a child how she would run her finger along its printed lines, reciting out loud those indecipherable letters which only pictographically she could identify as the name of God.

My grandmother spoke in proverbs and prayed audibly to Hanuman, the Hindu monkey-god, when he appeared on the movie screen; and when she counted money, it was according to the distinctive shapes and colors of the coins and bills. She was flexible, almost impatient with truth and so-called factual history and, like the contours of her life, her discussions were narrow, concrete, and frequently repeated: entreaties that we eat, stories about Partition [when India and Pakistan became independent of England colonialism in 1947], comments about the heat, or a panegyric to her sons. She was savvy, sage, and definitely crafty, but she also was not literate. Most of my life, I attributed these habits and idiosyncrasies to her "village mentality" or to that "traditional wisdom" about which people speak so reverently, almost sentimentally.[2]

Particularly important is the part of this passage—about my grandmother's ways of articulating herself and of comprehending and navigating the world. Because for so long I, like many others still across the globe, had mistaken or conflated this orally derived way of knowing with categories like "tradition," the "wisdom of the elders," or those frequently touted (but often amorphously elaborated) "culturally old ways." But my grandmother's mindset or mentality was no more influenced by her culture or point in history than by her engaging with the world foremost by way of her naked brain.

I say "foremost" because India at its national birth was completely mindful that millions of its citizens were not literate and, so, the government made allowances to assist them in "reading" their newly independent nation. India's differently colored

Figure 2.2 An old family photograph of the author as a child with her paternal grandmother, Jaswant Kaur Nayar. Courtesy of Rohan Kingwell.

and shaped bills and coins, for instance, were designed so that nonliterate Indians could tell one monetary unit from another, without having to rely on numbers alone. The pictorial symbols that appeared next to the written name of every party jostling for political power during elections were present expressly for those who could not read. Typists scattered across the market steps of Old Delhi could be hired to hammer out a letter or a contract that was recounted to them orally. Barkers, salesmen vocally pitching their wares, shop signs visualizing products: These were all means of communicating with customers who could *not* read letters. So, we need be careful *not* to presume that prelit, as a mentality of sorts, is exclusive to the past.

It's easy—too easy, really—for those of us ensconced in a culture that has naturalized writing to take that status for granted (think highway signs, TV news ticker tapes, and the ingredients listed on packaged food; think credit card bills and prescription-bottle instructions). The danger is, of course, that we may falsely perceive ourselves to be intrinsically "above" those who haven't naturalized writing, who function chiefly on the basis of their naked brains. We may consider ourselves naturally less prone toward communicating and thinking in ways that are cliche; naturally more likely to recognize nuance and accept ambiguity; naturally averse to viewing the world in a black-and-white way; and so, naturally, more likely to fall into the trap of believing, as even a sensitive soul like the author of *A Little History of Literature* can, that "[f]or most *thoughtful* people, literature will play a big part in their lives."[3] I've added the emphasis here for good reason. Is the intimation that people who cannot read, or who have been insufficiently trained in how to read literature, aren't thoughtful? If that is the case, then what kind of thought are we really talking about? Perhaps preferable is to say that a certain kind of thought-as-thoughtfulness is permitted emergence when the naked brain is able to engage with external technologies (alphabet, writing instrument, slate, paper, print). After all, it's those technologies that effectively allow for the production of this thing we call *literature*.

Notes

1 Ong, *Orality and Literacy*.
2 Nayar, *Cinematically Speaking*, 17.
3 Sutherland, *Little History*, 2.

References

Nayar, Sheila J. *Cinematically Speaking: The Orality-Literacy Paradigm for Visual Narrative*. New York: Hampton Press, 2010.

Ong, Walter J. *Orality and Literacy: The Technologizing of the Word*. London: Routledge, 1982.

Sutherland, John. *A Little History of Literature*. New Haven, CT: Yale University Press, 2013.

3 Existence without inscription

Some readers of this book may already be reeling at my eventually putting Bollywood cinema on epistemic par with epics produced by the likes of Homer. Indeed, I can already hear my rankled challenger who, not unlike myself, was probably doctrinally cultivated in the liberal arts tradition: "What? How possibly can you equate a masala formula film—the crude Hollywood of a 20th-century developing nation—with the grandeur of the *Iliad*? Bollywood spoken of in the same breath as *Beowulf*? That's—that's heresy!" So, how to denaturalize this potential state of (potentially haughtier) being? How to persuade skeptics of the possibility, at least, of some sort of storytelling correlation between ancient works of oral "poetry" and modern ones derided as "pulp" or crude popular culture "for the masses"? Even more, how to illustrate that these works inherently be underpinned by similar norms sufficiently enough to keep those skeptics—and maybe even you—reading this book?

There's actually a pretty quick way to shake off any assumptions that our postliteracy—and, even more, postprint—storytelling tradition inherently more sophisticated and refined than that of our oral predecessors or, worse, proof of our inborn superiority (rather than due to technologies in interanimation with our naked brains). I have used this method of conversion myself in the college classroom, as a route to getting students to engage more sympathetically with that most ancient of all extended narratives, the *Epic of Gilgamesh*. On a cold reading of that poem, students will often, and understandably, characterize it as "mythic," "episodic," "repetitive," sometimes even "weird," "cartoonish," "like the Old Testament," and "over the top." *Gilgamesh*, for those unfamiliar with the epic, recounts the adventures of a Sumerian king who not only fights beasts and downs forests, but who, on the loss of his friend, journeys to the underworld in the hopes of learning why humans must die. (So, weird and cartoonish maybe, but consider also how little has existentially changed in 5,000 years!) We'll come back to *Gilgamesh* time and again in what follows, including to address why I allege its being 5,000 years in age, when the most comprehensive version of that the epic we possess was only written down on clay tablets around 2,000 BCE.

As for that means of erasing students' unnatural indoctrination into literacy—which for most of them, has been occurring since they were infants via the ABCs, Mother Goose, and picture books like *Goodnight Moon*: The aid, intriguingly enough, derives from that youthful stage of life. Do you recall the childhood game Telephone, or Broken Telephone as I remember it? One child whispers something in an adjacent child's ear, with the utterance passed down until it reaches the ear of the final child in the group. That last child then recites out loud the transmitted message, which invariably sends players into peals of laughter, given how mangled and nonsensical the original message has become. My own students—doubtlessly as a respite from having to listen to their professor drone on—have always been keen and energetically willing to play; but, unlike the way the game is played in childhood, I ask participants to chat, to create a kind of white noise, before I lean in to whisper words into the first student's ear. Frequently, I give them the first line of Homer's *Odyssey*:

> *Tell me, Muse, of the ingenious and much-travelled man of many devices, who wandered full many ways after he had sacked the sacred citadel of Troy.*

"What?!" the initial player almost always quizzically exclaims. (Already the purity of that opening plea to the Muse is doomed.)

But down the lines of students the sentence travels—to arrive at the other end morphed into something like "Genie is a man of many ways"; or the more abrupt assertion, "Emus travel and wander"; or even, in stringier and less semantically clear fashion, "Tell the mouse is sick of sandwiches, oh boy." Yes, I'm more or less making these up right now, but you get the picture—and a garbled picture it always is, so much so that sometimes the end product comes delivered as a question.

Literate and literary as we may be—just imagine Nobel literature prize laureates such as Ernest Hemingway, John Steinbeck, Toni Morrison, and Orhan Pamuk collectively playing the game—communication breaks down with startling ease when it has to travel by word of mouth. And by no means are individuals invested in fields other than literature immune. Bruno Latour determined in a study of contemporary scientists that, when denied their instruments of inscription, the scientists

> "stuttered, hesitated, and talked nonsense, and displayed every kind of political or cultural bias. Although their minds, their scientific methods, their paradigms, their world-views and their cultures were still present, their conversation could not keep them in their proper place."[1]

In other words, it was *writing* and their practice of it that allowed those scientists to remain on track. No wonder that, millennia before, the ancient Greek playwright Aeschylus had, in his tragedy *Prometheus Bound*, referred to the invention of "put[ting] letters together" as "the memory of all things, mother of all the arts."

But to return to our hypothetical chain of Hemingway-Steinbeck-Morrison-Pamuk: Imagine those storytellers not only needing their material to travel from one person to the next through the space of the room, but also through time—that is, down the years, from one generation to the next, sometimes for centuries, as in the case of *Gilgamesh* before finally it got written down. This is when Broken Telephone proves particularly handy with students. After their playing, I ask them, "So, imagine now that you are a bard, an oral poet, a musician whose trade it is to mentally store and publicly share your community's saga (*saga*, incidentally derives from the Proto-Germanic word say). What will you have to do to your story to ensure its memorability? How are you going to make sure that knowledge about your community's gods and heroes and salient events will be conserved rather than endangered through time? What characters, what settings would most likely endure? Even more, what stories about your own tribe or nation or ethnic group would you deem *worth* saving—and why?" When students respond with their proposed catalog of attributes, what kinds of words and phrases do they ironically call to mind? "Mythic," "episodic," "repetitive," "cartoonish," "like the Old Testament," and "over the top." (We'll be investigating these characteristics more methodically and exegetically in the chapters that follow.)

Clearly, our naked brains are not like computer technology, which allows for the copying and pasting of huge swathes of information that can be sent intact with relative safety through space and time. In fact, according to psychologist and cognitive neuroscientist Merlin Donald, author of *Origins of the Modern Mind*, it's principally through reading and writing, as well as the graphic skills that append to literacy, that individuals become *like* computers:

> they are equipped to interface, to plug into whatever network becomes available. And once plugged in, their skills are determined by both the network and their own biological inheritance. Humans without such skills are isolated from the external memory system, somewhat like a computer that lacks the input/output devices needed to link up with a network.[2]

Of course, this networking happened, too, in the era of the printing press, albeit on a smaller and slower scale. But even earlier, ancient and medieval manuscripts written by hand acted as a kind of external storage system through which the past could be preserved—however inaccessible those works might have been outside the libraries, monasteries, and universities; however unstable or inaccurate the laborious copying process might have been.

Figure 3.1 The original external data storage of humankind. Courtesy
of the British Museum. The pictographic proto-cuneiform
depicted in this tablet, likely from southern Iraq (3,000 BCE),
may qualify as the earliest known writing. Today many of
us take literacy for granted, but imagine what it must have
been like when the human mind was finally freed from
the restrictions of having to remember all "data," such that
it could pursue new types of thought and modes of self-
expression. Even more, while you've likely been schooled
that "writing is rewriting," you can bet nobody was following
that maxim in the age of cuneiform, when the characters had
to be wedged onto clay tablets. (By the way, the data pressed
into this tablet records the allocation of beer.)

From this, we can certainly extrapolate how different and
also how *sophisticated*—even if in an entirely different way—
storytelling would have had to have been to survive in an oral
ecology. So deeply was this felt by Milman Parry, one of the
inaugural authorities on oral composition—he had spent time
in the 1930s studying Serbo-Croatian bards who were still orally
composing their heroic poetry—that he claimed that all human
literature fell into "two great parts"; and this was "not so much
because there are two kinds of culture, but because there are
two kinds of *form: one part of literature is oral, the other written*."[3]
More recently, the Albanian novelist Ismael Kadare proposed that

"In the history of literature there has been only one decisive change: the passage from orality to writing."[4]

Even the word *storytelling* becomes more rich and complicated in the prelit context. After all, oral narratives often functioned as storehouses for the entire span of their community's knowledge, which only writing, over the long haul, would allow to splinter and cascade out into autonomous disciplines: history, philosophy, astronomy, drama, political science, theology, and so forth. In earlier times, all that knowledge was bound together or, at the least, stored in ways less scientific or systematic than today, including in rituals and religion, in carvings to stoke memory, and in hero-driven songs. Just imagine having to carry in your head not only all the news of the day and your financial particulars, but also the particulars of all other humans you know, all places you know, everything that everyone in your community ever held dear, not to mention your entire ancestry and, of course, your gods. So, we need to be sensitive and extraordinarily vigilant regarding how literacy might impact what constitutes the "real," the "scientific," human "psychology," and even religious "truth." As we shall see—and as the classicist Eric Havelock once economically put it—what we communicate, and what we *can* communicate, alters substantially in an environment where knowers cannot be separated from what they know.[5]

Notes

1 Latour, "Visualization and Cognition," 4.
2 Donald, *Origins of the Modern*, 311.
3 Quoted in Scholes and Kellogg, *Nature of Narrative*, 18.
4 Kadare, interviewed by Shusha Guppy.
5 See in his book *Preface to Plato* chapter 6 especially, which is titled "Psyche or the Separation of the Knower from the Known" (197–214).

References

Donald, Merlin. *Origins of the Modern Mind: Three Stages in the Evolution of Culture and Cognition.* Cambridge, MA: Harvard University Press, 1991.

Havelock, Eric. *Preface to Plato*. Cambridge, MA: Belknap Press of Harvard University Press, 1963.

Kadare, Ismail. Interviewed by Shusha Guppy, in "Ismail Kadare, The Art of Fiction, No. 153," *The Paris Review*, 147 (Summer 1998), retrieved July 15, 2017, from www.theparisreview.org/interviews/1105/ismail-kadare-the-art-of-fiction-no-153-ismail-kadarefiction-no-153-ismail-kadare.

Latour, Bruno. "Visualization and Cognition: Thinking with Eyes and Hands," *Knowledge and Society: Studies in the Sociology of Culture Past and Present*, 6 (1986): 1–40.

Scholes, Robert, and Robert Kellogg. *The Nature of Narrative*. Oxford: Oxford University Press, 1968.

4 Myth and the mythical, epic and the epical

So, why are stories our foundational method of communication? Narratives, like life, as Roland Barthes exhorts, have always been with us: across all places, all periods, and all cultures. No society in the history of humanity has ever been found without them.[1] If we think about this through the lens of orality, the reasons for their universality become pretty clear. Without sufficiently flexible, accessible, and fixed external storage, what better means do we have to transport and communicate our communal self—our very humanity—through time?

Even more specifically, why, in their earliest incarnations, do such narratives often possess the qualities of myth? According to Merriam-Webster's primary definition of the term, a myth is "a usually traditional story of ostensibly historical events that serves to unfold part of the world view of a people or explain a practice, belief, or natural phenomenon."[2] Perhaps already you've caught some of the unintended orality-related giveaways here—in grammatical units like "traditional," "ostensibly historical," and "worldview of a people." But does this mean that myths were taken by oral cultures as, well, *mythical*? That is, did those cultures consider their myths to be myths in the way that we moderns typically conceive of the term—as representative of stories that are imaginary or overly fabulous?

The etymology of the word *myth* is extremely revealing. While those who study the history of words cannot account for its exact origins, thanks to Douglas Harper's superb online etymology dictionary, I can at least tell you that the ancient Greek word *mythos* meant "speech, thought, story, myth, anything delivered by word of mouth."[3] Certainly, the references here to "speech" and "delivered by word of mouth" are telling. No wonder that, while literature arrived only relatively recently on the scene, myth has been with us from the beginning. In fact, given our hundreds of thousands of years as preliterate humans, one wonders if over time we became wired to think mythically. John Sutherland suggests so, likening that wiring to the sort linguists argue neurologically occurs in infants with respect to learning language. "Myth-making," declares Sutherland, "is in our nature. It's part of who we are as human beings."[4]

Yet, too often we contemporarily associate mythmaking with something in the negative. Frequently the word is employed and thereby conjures something untrue or untrustworthy: an implication of confabulation, of exaggeration or, worse yet, of outright lying. But I ask once more: Would our oral predecessors have considered this to be the case, or is it more that we readers, so removed now from the pressures that orality places on story-telling, have downgraded myth and aligned it with the fictional? Oral traditions may feel texturally mythic, but that doesn't mean they don't carry truth—certainly not a truth any more or less contrived than our own literacy-motivated categorization of the past according to (made-up) dates and times.

When your entire tribal history has to be carried by word of mouth, moreover, wouldn't you be more inclined to privilege, pre-serve, and pass on your *inheritance* of tribally relevant personages, places, and events rather than to concoct stories out of thin air, as is the wont of novelists? In fact, when studied intimately, myths, it turns out, not only track the astronomical world, they also describe travel routes and report on disputes with rival tribes; they explicate the origins of things and one's relationship to one's gods; they contemplate human mortality, record past gift exchanges, tell stories to appease rage and to manage conflict (and, so, hope-fully, too, to marshal conciliation); and finally—only because this sentence is now long enough—they vocally map the tribal past, recalling especially formidable events like floods and wars.

And yet, *still* these stories may sound too concocted to our literate ears to qualify as history. Either they're past events precariously trapped in fictions—or, worse, outright fictions, given their affinity for histrionics (too hysterical!), hyperbole (so exaggerated! so impossible!), and anthropomorphization (non-human things treated like people!). Sometimes, here, archaeology helps us out. Consider, for instance, the case of excavations done on Triquet Island, which lies off the coast of British Columbia, Canada. For generations, the Heiltsuk Nation orally recounted a story about their ancestors having sought refuge on an unfrozen island along what is now Canada's western coast. This they had done, so the oral history said, in order to survive the last Ice Age. As you can imagine, the story was often regarded as a "creation myth," which is to say a fancifully symbolic narrative about both the world's and a people's origins. Well, as it turns out, recent radiocarbon dating suggests that human settlement on Triquet Island goes back some 14,000 years—which was precisely when most of Canada was gelidly slumbering under glaciers.[5] Consider what this means time-wise: That story had passed through *350 consecutive lifetimes!*

Discoveries of cities such as Troy likewise bear out that what may sound like mere fiction often hinges on an authentic bygone event, albeit one that has had to be protractedly transmitted through oral communication alone. (If archaeological finds such as these speak to the crucial relations between oral history and science, they also pay sad tribute to how peoples' myths are often only deemed valid or authentic on the basis of that science—which is, of course, entirely a byproduct of literacy, both alphabetical and numerical.) How a factual event or genuine encounter may have *had* to be contorted in order to survive passage through the ages is precisely what we will be examining later on in these pages; and it's an examination that will hopefully mitigate our perhaps too-swift demotion of myth or, if not quite that, at least our inclination to view it only on aesthetic terms, as poetry for poetry's sake.

Considering everything that storytelling in the oral context had to carry—all history, all ancestry, all knowledge of agriculture, of the seasons, of the earth and the stars and the seas, of one's enemies and one's friends—we should likewise be cautious about equating such storytelling with the "primitive." Recall what happened to those scientists Latour studied, or to my own students when playing Broken Telephone. Deny ourselves inscription, force us into an exclusively oral scenario, and watch how quickly our capacity to retain and pass on communicated information falls apart. To compose and transmit an oral story through time involves a very complex set of activities and skills, and a very different economy of thought—which we'll additionally address in the ensuing chapters.

Then again, anthropologist Claude Levi-Strauss suggested that what myths really embody are those stories we *live by*[6]—implying that, for us today, these might constitute things like nation, religion, God, scientific truth. (If you're thinking, *No—not true! The latter are different—they are real!*, then Levi-Strauss' point has been made.) What this nuancing of myth additionally points to is how we will have to be very careful as we proceed about teasing away mythic elements that derive necessarily—which is to say, for epistemic reasons—from other mythic elements that get incorporated as a style. Some might describe a film such as Ang Lee's film *Crouching Tiger, Hidden Dragon* and a novel such as Cormac McCarthy's *Blood Meridian* as "mythic," but they certainly aren't so because of their investment in an oral way of knowing or any requirement that they reach an audience predisposed toward orality.

A similar sort of problem arises with respect to *epic*. Today, we bandy that word about fairly widely and loosely—as in the description of two sports teams taking part in an "epic battle," or of an adventurous day of skiing as having been "epic." In terms of literature, more particularly, a book critic might refer to Herman Melville's *Moby Dick* as "a great American epic," while bewailing another novel for its unnecessarily epical length or overreach. In all these cases, the word has been seized from its initial (and initially oral) context to become more a designation of a work's scope, or size, or national bearing.

In its strictest definitional sense, epic applies to a very specific and very ancient set of texts that are "heroic" in tone. These are stories that recount a hero's adventures in a very elevated, lofty, or magnanimous style that matches that hero's larger-than-life persona. For some of you, Homeric epic may spring immediately to mind—as should now, too, the tellingly titled *Epic of Gilgamesh*. (And, yes, heroism in these times was decidedly masculine, so one finds no epical heroines akin to, say, Sigourney Weaver's rendering of Ripley in the *Alien* films.)

Once again, etymology offers us an enlightening clue regarding what epic was at its inception. Notwithstanding the contemporary bagginess of the word, the Greek *epikos*, from *epos*, signified a word, tale, or prophecy; a story, proverb, or promise; or poetry in heroic verse. If that seems to you no less definitionally baggy, know that that Greek word derives from the Proto-Indo-European (PIE) root *wekw-*, "to speak" (the * denotes that PIE is a reconstructed parent language). Certainly, this linguistic root sheds some light on why, while the word *epic* may still be with us, the actual production of it, our capacity to generate a great epic as was done in the past, has become less and less feasible. For, an epic was not a creative telling of a story so much as it was a creative *re*telling of a story. And so, as we shall soon see, there are some pretty good reasons—orality-related reasons—why the epic as a living and successful literary genre eventually waned.

Notes

1 Yuval Noah Harari contends in *Sapiens* that during the foraging era of *Homo sapiens*—that is, before the Agricultural Revolution some 10,000 years ago—cooperation between hundreds of strangers, who might come across each other while in their small bands, was only possible because of their shared myths. He also postulates that when that Agricultural Revolution did come, the crowded cities and mighty empires that ensued led to people "invent[ing] stories about great gods, motherlands and joint stock companies to provide the needed social links" (115). Shared myths, in other words, sustained empires—oftentimes oppressively and exploitatively.
2 Myth, in *Merriam-Webster's Collegiate Dictionary* (n.d.), retrieved from www.merriam-webster.com/dictionary/myth.
3 Harper, *Online Etymology Dictionary*. All etymological explanations that follow are from this extremely rich website.

4 Sutherland, *Little History*, 7.
5 Katz, "Found."
6 See, for instance, his book *Myth and Meaning*.

References

Harari, Yuval Noah. *Sapiens: A Brief History of Humankind*. New York: Random House, 2015.

Harper, Douglas. *Online Etymology Dictionary*, 2001–2019. Retrieved July 15, 2019, from www.etymonline.com.

Katz, Brigit. "Found: One of the Oldest Settlements," 5 April 2017, *Smithsonian.com*. Retrieved July 17, 2017, from www.smithsonianmag. com/smart-news/one-oldest-north-american-settlements-found-180962750/.

Lévi-Strauss, Claude. *Myth and Meaning: Cracking the Code of Culture*. New York: Random House, 1995.

Merriam-Webster's Collegiate Dictionary. Retrieved July 17, 2017, from https://www.merriam-webster.com/dictionary/.

Sutherland, John. *A Little History of Literature*. New Haven, CT: Yale University Press, 2013.

5 Why prelit matters

Some of the rationale for this book is doubtlessly evident to you based on the preceding sections. But I want to mention a few additional reasons why a book on what came before literature matters. First is that it offers a foundational way for those of us who regularly engage with literature, whether in the classroom or on our own, to think more capaciously about the nature of narrative. Too often, we intellectually detach written storytelling from its origins in the spoken word. By not attending to what narrative in the oral milieu often *had* to be paradigmatically—which is to say, as a pattern, as set of relations—we lose sight of where literacy allowed storytelling to go. (Incidentally, the word "paradigm" comes from the Greek *paradeiknunai*, "to show side by side"—from *para-* ["beside"] and *deiknunai* ["to show"].) In fact, by familiarizing ourselves with the characteristics that often drive oral composition, we also become better equipped to determine, discern, and more suggestively hypothesize characteristics of storytelling that were inventively wrought by the alphabet. Sometimes those characteristics might even prove writing's outright offspring, born of the radical capacity for knowers to be separate from what they know. Inscription, as aforementioned, could now serve as an extension of the brain, as an external storage drive that freed human minds from the task of being a memory bank.

Studying literature without attending to *pre*literature is thus a bit like studying the current makeup of diabetes or high blood pressure without attending to that disease's etiology, to its origins or causes. That's why I earlier referred to this book as addressing prelit, given the purposeful way that that term invokes the familiar "premed." Premed, of course, alludes to the preliminary coursework and relevant scientific knowledge base that students need in advance of entering medical school: organic chemistry, physics, biology, and the like. Only through these means can future doctors legitimately attend to the particulars of medicine and what constitutes both healthy and diseased human bodies. So, while many a college literature course today focuses almost exclusively on the novel, that, in my mind, is a bit like that doctor giving the patient with diabetes the latest medicine, but without any notion of what causes the disease on the cellular level—and, so, of how and why that particular medicine works.

Robert Scholes and Robert Kellogg lamented almost 40 years ago our modern culture's "novel-centered view of narrative literature."[1] For them, this was unfortunate primarily because the novel cut readers off from so many literatures and cultures of the past. While the novel represents several centuries of the tradition of continuous narrative, that tradition, in written form, goes back four thousand years! Obviously, the novel is a relatively recent arrival—as are, accordingly, the thought and habits that accompany its particular breed of symbolic invention. Myth, by contrast, has been with us for eternity.

Perhaps some numerical elaborations will help to drive this integral point home. Arrowheads date humanity's interaction with technology to 200,000 years ago, which, given when cuneiform emerged, means that we were more or less exclusively oral creatures for 195,000 years. Even the more modest suggestion by some paleontologists of 100,000 of human articulated language means about 4,750 successive generations of oral storytelling. The most generous aggregate of generations of alphabetically literate culture, meanwhile, chalks in at 250 generations.

What is more, written continuous narrative emerged *from* the oral tradition, as Scholes and Kellogg point out.[2] So, if we are willing to spend a little time exploring the hows and whys of the characteristics of oral narrative, we will, as readers, be able to identify and interpret in much more nuanced and enticing fashion when literature was (and, on occasion, still is) maintaining and perpetuating—sometimes consciously, sometimes not—that more ancient way of knowing. Cutting textuality off from its roots, starting with and from the exclusively *text*-bound—as if novels or modern drama somehow sprouted intact like Athena from Zeus's head—obscures the much fuller, wider, and more holistically and historically grounded story of narrative. Walter J. Ong went so far as to suggest that poststructuralist thinkers who played with text in this more myopic fashion—he was thinking particularly of Jacques Derrida—were engaging in a kind of "occultism," one "endlessly titillating" perhaps, but "not especially informative."[3] Why? Because theorists who focused on the instability of meaning inherent in writing did so by ignoring the stability of meaning toward which those without inscription are more inclined. As an example of this stability—and as a preview of what is explanatorily to follow—think of all those clichés, proverbs, and platitudes from your childhood: "white as snow," "dumb as a doornail," "knock on wood," "don't count your chickens before they're hatched." While writers today may consider these rhetorically stale and unsophisticated, such means of expression were—and remain, for reasons of efficiency and economy—instrumental to securing meaning orally through time.

In this sense, academic fields of literature could be gently accused of having fallen prey to their own literacy. While humanities departments today eagerly support subdisciplines such as the History of the Book, the Materiality of the Book and, in more recent decades, Digital Humanities—all worthwhile areas of study, to be sure—they are less likely, sometimes neglectful and, in more despairing cases, unreceptive to acknowledging our collective oral heritage, as well as the pressures that may continue to weigh on narrative when in its prelit form. Here, I mean narratives such as those Bollywood movies I introduced earlier, which can continue to function on the basis of oral modes of narrativity.[4] Consider, additionally, that the fast-developing field of cognitive science as related to narrative (e.g., book reading, film viewing) continues to be built foremost on the study of two kinds of minds, both of them highly specialized: that of the computer, and that of the literate English-speaking adult.

As Merlin Donald said in 1991—and, sadly, what he said still applies today in spite of his ambition to rectify the situation—"Cognitive science often carries on as though humans had no culture, no significant variability, and no history."[5] In short, his hypothesis was that, when it came to the organization of the mind, computational approaches to language needed to attend as much to the human development of memory technologies as they did to biological or genetically encoded factors in our evolution: "Humans did not simply evolve a larger brain, an expanded memory, a lexicon, or a special speech apparatus; we evolved new systems for representing reality."[6] So, it surely makes sense that we who study and engage with literature—or, even more broadly, who take intellectual stock in the humanities—benefit by taking account of the various systems that our species developed for representing reality prior to the novel. Why begin only with the book? Why privilege the materiality of literary production when, for most of our human evolution, we had to rely chiefly on immaterial means for producing and passing on our stories, our history, and those events that gave us collective meaning and purpose? Any theory of narrativity is shortsighted if it disregards the history and phenomenology bound up with oral narrativity. (*Phenomenology*, in this instance, means how narrativity is experienced by individuals; after all, even today, one person engaging with a story may have undergone 20 years of literacy education while another, of the same age, may have experienced none—and, so, is operating basically by oral means.)

Some of you may well be asking: But haven't all the stories in our current possession—*especially* those from the remotest past—been reworked by the hands of literate folk and put into book form? And of course, you would be absolutely correct. But consider that, at the last annual Modern Language Association conference which I attended, in 2017—this is a conference where thousands of academics of literatures and languages gather to present and hear literally thousands of papers—not a single panel attended to orality's sway on literature, not even at those sessions that were *about* the history of literature. Indeed, in an encounter I had with one academic on this subject, I was told, "I was taught during the 1980s when I was in graduate school not to take such approaches seriously." (I should probably mention that it was in the 1980s that the poststructuralist thought of Derrida was at its most fashionable.)

Remember my earlier conjecture that many intellectuals in highly industrialized societies may have had—through no fault of their own—very little in the way of intimate, long-term encounters with non literate adults who reside in nonliterate subcultures? Remember also my saying that, consequently, they may associate orality with something past or even "backward"? (In fact, the same may well apply to you!) Just as possible, and certainly more uncomfortable, is that we may be reluctant to acknowledge or probe too deeply the class-related biases inherent in our own acquisition of what educators call *high literacy*. In short, high literacy hinges on skills like the ability to infer and impose meaning, to make nuanced judgments, to deal with uncertainty, and to read against the grain (all which, of course, we have to be taught). Some of us may also be afraid, or at least disinclined, to give orality its due for reasons of political correctness that are, in actual fact, self-interestedly motivated. That is, referring to an entire culture, subculture, or even an individual as "fundamentally oral" may be perceived as a taint, as an insinuation of an individual or culture's lesser status—while simultaneously drawing uncomfortable attention to the fact that the ones doing the judging are often (or, at least, perceive themselves to be) highly removed from that epistemic state. As a result, we may be eager, as that aforementioned academic was, to counter orality, and to highlight instead traces of literacy that exist in disparate cultures and individuals. But are we really being humanistic by ignoring or denying alternative ways of knowing, in demanding that others be more like ourselves? One could argue that dismissing orality altogether signals a tacit belief that the literate self is superior and maybe even, quite hazardously, "complete."

But orality by no means implies *in*completion as a way of being. All of us as children were cognitively oral, after all, until some of us were weaned from that state of being at the age of four, five, or six. And while an oral way of knowing may no longer reflect the symbolic language integral to *your* sense of being (given that you are reading this book), it is a way of thought and expression through which individuals are fully able to cope with the demands of living—that is, until the world around them insists on molding and organizing itself on the basis of literacy. Hence the alphabetic, as opposed to pictorial, signs that dot our highways and storefronts, and the tags in our clothes, and the ones on our groceries—not to mention, the news ticker that runs along the bottom of so many informational TV broadcasts, and the fact that you are engaging with the concept of orality by way of a book entitled *Before Literature*.

Ignoring orality does not make us more ethical as thinkers. In fact, in my mind, ignoring orality is comparable to our turning a blind eye to the millions who are today without clean water, electricity, or sufficient food, in order to satisfy our projection of the world as technologically advanced, globalized, and even posthuman. Additionally, while our current openness in the educational arena to diversity is admirable, why does that diversity encompass sensitivity to gender, sexuality, ethnicity, religion, and disability, but not to orality—which is so often intertwined with issues of class and socio-economic position? We might even say that orality as a way of knowing, if not quite a tradition any longer, has been driven underground by our dominant writing culture. So, I consider it my task to bring that oral way of knowing to your consciousness, so that you, as readers, can become smarter and more sensitive to the multiple ways of knowing that dot our global landscape. In some sense, this book seeks to return the oral to a level of status parallel with that of the literate. Recall that medical education cannot exist without premedical education; and while the medical may be perceived as more sophisticated because it is built on or evolves out of the premedical, that in some sense makes the premedical—and so, too, the oral—*more* germane, not less. The former could never exist without that more foundational scaffold, much as an oak seed cannot propagate the oak species without first establishing its oak-tree roots.

In order for you to really grasp the nature of both oral and alphabetically literate ways of knowing—as well as their capacities for complex interplay—I need to introduce you to two evolutionary concepts as applied to learning. (Just so you know, this is the most technical part of the entire book. So, do get ready—but know also that the remainder of the book *isn't* going to weigh on your brain quite drily as this section might.) The first concept is that of *phylogeny*, which entails what we have learned collectively over time. In other words, you could hardly learn the language Hindi or Spanish had it not developed and been passed down through the centuries, complete with evolving rules of syntax, a particular vocabulary, a script with diacritical marks, and so on. (In linguistics, this is referred to as *diachronic* development.) The second and related concept is *ontogeny*, implying the evolution of our individual learning during our lifespan. In this case, we're referring to an infant who learns to speak her mother tongue of Hindi or Spanish, then to read it as a toddler, then to write it with ever-increasing skill.

Even the best of intellectuals can fall into the trap of overstating one of these evolutionary developments while ignoring the other. One of the greatest historians of this century, Lucien Febvre, himself endeavored, as micro-historian Carlo Ginzburg tells it, "to distinguish the mental coordinates of an entire age on the basis of studying a single individual, albeit a very exceptional one—Rabelais."[7] (For those unfamiliar with François Rabelais, he was the 16th-century French writer of the scurrilous but also scholarly novel *Gargantuan and Pantagruel.*) In short, because Febvre projected the "notion of a classless 'collective mentality,'" his research on what was actually "a narrow stratum of French society composed of cultivated individuals [was] extended by implication, with no one excepted, to encompass an entire century."[8] One mentality for all, as it were—notwithstanding that Rabelais hardly reflected the epistemic norm of the 1500s. More accurately, he was its ontogenetic exemplar.

If, as brain science has shown, humans are incapable of reasoning or even thinking without emotions—which is to say, without narratives—wouldn't that organically mandate different kinds of narratives that appeal and attend to people's different epistemic locations apropos orality and literacy? In other words, we should pretty much anticipate that stories for those who had been onto-genetically cultivated like Rabelais might coexist with stories for those who had been denied any immersion in letters. True, according to some cognitive scientists, even today's non literate individual (I resist using the term *illiterate*, to which they them-selves are not immune) must depend on channels of experience that are exographic, that are outside the self rather than dependent on biological memory. Because of media like television, these scientists argue, the non literate individual's channels of experi-ence are bound up with material symbols that are external to their being. But as we shall soon see, sometimes an oral way of knowing can be paradigmatically housed *in* those outside channels, par-ticularly visual ones that can circumvent the alphabetic literacy required to read a book, or even a graphic novel or webpage.

For those who are more science-oriented: Remember that the changes induced by alphabetic literacy aren't only external; they're also internal, as in physiological. Literacy quite literally changes the circuitry of the brain—and "drastically," at that, as cognitive neuroscientist Stanislas Dehaene puts it.[9] In a recent study in India, 21 women from the northern city of Lucknow, most of whom could not recognize even a word of Hindi, were taught to read. Within six months, they had achieved a first-grade proficiency in its written script known as Devanagari. The brain scans that followed startled the German, Indian, and Netherlander scientists who had designed the project. Areas deep below the cortices of these new readers had changed. Why was this startling? Because the majority of reading-related brain activity was assumed to involve reorganization of the cortex alone. But even the more ancient regions of the brain—ones we share with mice and other mammals—were impacted. The senior author of the group, Falk Huettig, of the Max Planck Institute for Psycholinguistics in Germany, had this to say regarding the "rela-tively young phenomenon of human literacy":

> The first proper scripts were invented less than 6,000 years ago. That means there is no reading area or reading network

that could be specified in our genes. Looking at *how cultural inventions change brain function and structures* helps us to understand how the brain works on a fundamental level.[10]

(I've added the emphasis here, and hopefully you can see why.) Huettig also worthily reminds us of something I've already mentioned, which is that the incapacity to read alphabetically is not exclusive to the developing world. Millions of individuals in the United States, for instance, are "functionally illiterate," meaning that they "struggle to read even very simple sentences."[11]

So, in order to comprehend literacy's sway on us individually (ontogenetically), we benefit by starting *before* literacy. Think of the oral norms of narrative as constituting a kind of human storytelling baseline. Even more, in extracting what narrative is—and sometimes had or has to be—before the influence and imposition of alphabetic literacy, we will apprehend with greater clarity how literacy alters not only storytelling's structure and content, but also the content and orientation of our human brains. Somewhat unavoidably, we will also tackle what constitutes all manner of criteria when it comes to storytelling, including thematic criteria (the kinds of messages that are culturally expressed); functional criteria (how forms of narrativity "work"); quantitative criteria (the extent to which these forms are diffused throughout society); and, perhaps most significantly, aesthetic criteria (what comprises "good," "beautiful," or "superior" storytelling).

So, after finishing *Before Literature*, not only will you be conversant with the what, how, and wherefore of the oral characteristics of narrative; you will also, once more, be able to detect—or, at least, to conjecture with greater acuity—some of the same for the structure, content, and form of alphabetically literate narrative. More to the point of this book, you will be forced to rethink in part the allegations made by critics that the "culture industry"— commercially marketed and standardized popular culture, such as mass-marketed movies and TV programs—inherently turns spectators into passive receptors. (This was the claim famously made in the 1940s by the cultural theorists Theodor Adorno and Max Horkheimer of the Frankfurt School.) Once exposed to

what drives the oral episteme and why, you may have additionally to renegotiate the interpretive filters that literate scholars
sometimes bring to the study of narrative. After all, if a reader, as
Roland Barthes famously claimed, is a composite of all that she
has read or even imagined as written,[12] what of that "reader"—as,
say, of movies or TV programs—who is exclusively oral?

Notes

1 Scholes and Kellogg, *Nature of Narrative*, 8.
2 Ibid., 9.
3 Ong, *Orality and Literacy*, 169–170.
4 I use the word *narrativity* rather than *narratology*, as the latter has been
   conceived as a branch of poetics, as an extension of formalism even.
   My project, on the other hand, is more broadly concerned with how
   narratives "work"; and—in the case of *Before Literature*'s more exclusive focus on oral narrativity—with how narratives generate meaning
   and render that meaning both comprehensible and transmissible.
5 Donald, *Origins of the Modern*, 1.
6 Ibid., 3.
7 Ginzburg, *Cheese and the Worms*, xxiii.
8 Ibid.
9 Dehaene, *Reading in the Brain*, 208.
10 This appears in Gary Stix's *Scientific American* article "The Illiterate
   Adult, Learning to Read Produces Enormous Brain Changes."
11 Equally concerning in the American context is the "seemingly
   intractable gap," as Wolf argues, "between many, more privileged
   European-American students and many, less privileged African-
   American and Hispanic students" (Wolf, *Tales of Literacy*, 38).
12 See especially Barthes' *The Pleasure of the Text*.

References

Barthes, Roland. *The Pleasure of the Text*. New York: Farrar, Strauss &
   Giroux, 1975.
Dehaene, Stanislas. *Reading in the Brain: The New Science of How We Read*.
   New York: Penguin Books, 2010.
Donald, Merlin. *Origins of the Modern Mind: Three Stages in the Evolution
   of Culture and Cognition*. Cambridge, MA: Harvard University Press,
   1991.

Ginzburg, Carlo. *The Cheese and the Worms: The Cosmos of a Sixteenth-Century Miller*. Trans. John and Anne Tedeschi. Baltimore: Johns Hopkins University Press, 1980.

Ong, Walter J. *Orality and Literacy: The Technologizing of the Word*. London: Routledge, 1982.

Scholes, Robert, and Robert Kellogg. *The Nature of Narrative*. Oxford: Oxford University Press, 1968.

Stix, Gary. "The Illiterate Adult, Learning to Read Produces Enormous Brain Changes." *Scientific American*, May 24, 2017. Retrieved from https://blogs.scientificamerican.com/talking-back/for-the-illiterate-adult-learning-to-read-produces-enormous-brain-changes/.

Wolf, Maryanne. *Tales of Literacy for the 21st Century*. Oxford: Oxford University Press, 2016.

6   But there is always a *but* ...

Analyzing storytelling from the vantage point of orality may be valuable, but one also has to be extremely careful not to project orality as the binary opposite of alphabetic literacy—a projection that is far too facile and sometimes even philosophically dangerous. (That bit of wisdom we owe gratefully to Jacques Derrida.) Yes, on the surface, it may appear as if I'm promoting some sort of split or "great dichotomy," as anthropologist Jack Goody once phrased it,[1] with everything appearing exclusively on one side or the other of that divide: oral *or* literate; written *or* spoken; modern *or* traditional. In truth, the picture is far more complicated than that (which may explain why Goody was accused of perpetuating that divide at the same time that he was trying theoretically to undo it). Literate culture bleeds into oral culture. The novelist draws on the man of no letters to create a character like Sancho Panza in *Don Quixote*. The traditional not only meets the modern but also adapts some of the latter's cultural practices. Consider, as a single colorful example, that the oral Yugoslav poets recorded in the early twentieth century by Milman Parry made explicit mention in their songs of such written documents as telegrams![2]

Obviously, humankind's relationship to the spoken, as well as to the written word, never stops changing. Equally essential to bear in mind is that the introduction of writing into an area of a culture doesn't immediately introduce anything like literacy in its modern sense. That, as we have already noted, requires an established educational tradition based in letters. But in order for us to appreciate the extent to which literate narrative has the potential (and "luxury") to depart from exclusively oral narrative, we need at least a threshold for the latter, a boundary, or what earlier I referred to as an oral-storytelling baseline; we require some sort of paradigmatic reference point—never forgetting, of course, that a paradigm implies a model, a pattern, *not* a set of strict, inflexible, and unalterable rules.

Consequently, we will need to isolate—or "excavate," in the social theorist Michel Foucault's manner of speaking—those norms most fundamental to the oral episteme of narrative. We will have to tease out the characteristics that comprise, often in reticulate, or interconnected, fashion, a communal narrative transmitted and received on the basis of exclusively oral/aural means. True, to some degree this is as an intellectual exercise, and a slightly artificial one, at that. Not only is this because inscription in the form of nicks, symbols, pictographs, and so forth has long been present in oral communities, but because most of the orally derived narratives we possess, as earlier I mentioned, only exist because the performances of them were lodged in writing. As a result, they may oftentimes bear some unconscious tidying-up—material evidence, if caught, of the structural, formal, and even stylistic or aesthetic "toilette" exacted on them by their literate amanuenses. The distinctions *in situ* between the oral and the literate are consequently nowhere near as crisp or exactly constituted as I'm going to present them here, though they *are* grounded in a significant body of scholarly work.

In other words, my assemblage of these orally inflected traits, which we shall (finally!) begin examining next chapter, owes everything to the steady and concerted research performed by numerous anthropologists, classicists, social psychologists, medieval and Renaissance scholars, religion scholars, literary theorists, historians, and experts in film and media studies. The constituents of this paradigm have by no means been pulled out of thin air. I will also be providing you numerous examples drawn from both past and relatively recent sources—Homeric epics, Hindu epics, fairy tales, ballads, formula films—not only to justify but to exemplify how these oft-reticulated norms operate, sometimes even surviving relatively intact *within* print culture. Yes, mixing in fairy tales and movies with grand epics like the *Odyssey* or the *Mahabharata* may still seem to some of my readers inappropriate, if not downright sacrilegious. Then again, shouldn't we expect to find a multiplicity of storytelling forms inhabiting the oral realm (lofty epics preserving a people's history, fables told around the hearth), much as we can find a mix of literatures in the print realm (pulp fiction, literary fiction, children's books)?

As for why I am also including movies here, let me reprise my rationale—only this time by drawing on the work of another scholar. In his groundbreaking *Highbrow/Lowbrow*, the American historian Lawrence Levine drew attention to how literacy encroached upon the pervasively oral culture of the immigrants who arrived on the shored of the United States in the late nineteenth and early twentieth centuries. This was an audience accustomed to listening, not reading, and, so, a ready constituency for the visual entertainments that defined the era: sports like baseball and boxing, theatrical productions like vaudeville and burlesque—but *especially* (and, here, the emphasis is Levine's) "the new silent movies, which could be enjoyed by larger and often more marginal audiences less steeped in the language and the culture" of America.[3] As my own research regarding the blueprint for the twentieth-century Indian formula film has borne out, immigrants to America were not the only ones, culturally speaking, for whom movies could operate as an extension or adaptation of oral narratives. While Levine may have highlighted not orality but listening alone vis-a-vis the audiences of those motion pictures—ironic, perhaps, given that the movies were basically silent until 1929—their structure and style are often very much in keeping with the characteristics of traditionally oral narrative (something I've discussed at length in an essay entitled "Seeing Voices: Oral Pragmatics and the Silent Cinema"[4]).

But before we proceed with our detailed investigation of the characteristics that undergird the oral episteme of narrative, first a point I made earlier that merits reaffirming—namely, that episteme's boundaries are porous, not unassailable. True, the oral episteme may reflect our more "natural" mode of storytelling, but it also remains a theoretical model subject to flow and variance ("like that [border] between Tijuana and San Diego," as Bruno Latour argues with respect to what divides prescientific from scientific culture).[5] While useful for teaching—hence my reliance on it here—in actuality, no split exists between the written and the oral that is this tidy or simple, just as there it doesn't between subject and object, or self and community (or science and prescience). Still, ignoring or intellectually jettisoning half of the equation by homing in exclusively on the written (or subject, or self, or science) doesn't necessarily serve as an illuminating remedy or rectification either.

So, with all that said, let us begin our exploration and exposition of what constitutes an epistemically oral narrative; and let us start with why such narrative often *has* to be assembled in a certain way.

Notes

1 Goody, *Domestication of the Savage Mind*.
2 For an excellent archive to the work of Milman Parry and his mentee Albert Lord (also the first curator of that archive), visit the "Milman Parry Collection of Oral Literature On-Line," which you can retrieve at https://mpc.chs.harvard.edu//.
3 Levine, *Highbrow/Lowbrow*, 47.
4 See Nayar, "Seeing Voices."
5 Latour, "Visualization," 2.

References

Goody, Jack. *The Domestication of the Savage Mind*. Cambridge: Cambridge University Press, 1977.

Latour, Bruno. "Visualization and Cognition: Thinking with Eyes and Hands," *Knowledge and Society: Studies in the Sociology of Culture Past and Present*, 6 (1986): 1–40.

Levine, Lawrence W. *Highbrow/Lowbrow: The Emergence of Cultural Hierarchy in America*. Cambridge, MA: Harvard University Press, 1988.

Milman Parry Collection, © 2012. Retrieved July 18, 2017, at https://mpc.chs.harvard.edu//.

Nayar, Sheila J. "Seeing Voices: Oral Pragmatics and the Silent Cinema," *Early Popular Visual Culture* 7, 2 (2009): 145–165.

7 A beginning with no definitive beginning

Let's begin by imaginarily returning to the classroom where my students have just taken part in that game of Broken Telephone. For, after initiating them into the pressures that orality can place on communicating (even a single line of) story, I engage them in another exercise; and I do so primarily to stimulate their own discernment of traits that might be intrinsic to a narrative when composed and transmitted exclusively by word of mouth. This exercise entails asking a student, who is publicly willing to endure potential embarrassment, to recount for the class a story they remember from their earliest days. My only instructions are that the story be one with which most, if not all, of us are familiar, and one that they remember less as something read than as something *told*. Typically, the tale of choice is "Goldilocks and the Three Bears" or "Little Red Riding Hood." While on the surface my request may appear an invitation for the performance of something silly or childish, my reasons for requesting a story from their earliest. years are actually quite judicious. They're certainly not born of my wanting students to equate orality with a state of innocence or intellectual juvenility. Rather, I solicit a story from their youth because childhood is the period—at least, in the customary context of industrialized societies—*before* humans are inculcated into a literate way of thinking, into a mentality contoured by reading and writing. As a result, these are the stories that are most likely to bear still the imprint of oral inflection.

And how do these stories almost invariably start? How does practically every student willing to endure the pressures of a recitation begin? With *Once upon a time* … As in, Once upon a time, there was a girl named Little Red Riding Hood … Or, Once upon a time, there lived three bears, a Papa Bear, a Mama Bear, and a Baby Bear … And, Once upon a time, there lived in the forest … Once upon a time, there was a great ruler … Once upon a time, when animals could talk … Once upon a time, a long time ago, the Everything-Maker was very busy … We've all heard such openings, probably dozens of time over. And we've also all probably subsequently been told *not* to use them in our writing because of their being commonplace or cliché—stock phrases too overused and, hence, unoriginal.

And, indeed, unoriginal they are. Or, if we prefer a description with less negative associations: Variants of these phrases come with a long and relatively universal history. We can find them in Chinese ("A very, very long time ago …"); German ("Back in the days …"); Hindi ("It's an old story …"); Icelandic ("Once there was …"); Irish ("A long, long, long time ago …"); Latin ("At that time, once …"); and Tagalog ("Back in the old time …"). (Check out "Once upon a time" on Wikipedia for an even more extensive library reflecting the historically transnational breadth of this pat expression.)

So, what accounts for the relative omnipresence of "Once upon a time …" at the outset of fairy tales, fables, and ancient myths? Why would so many narratives across so many disparate cultures begin in this identical fashion? And what, at the same time, accounts for our (somewhat forced) contemporary dislike, and even dismissal, of this opening—and here I mean beyond its smacking of something cliche? In the simplest terms, for individuals inculcated into a literate mindset, beginning a story with "Once upon a time …" draws immediate attention, even if only subconsciously, to our preliterate way of knowing, to the altogether historically opaque or cloudy nature of the past when we existed (or exist still) in an oral milieu.

Okay, so maybe those terms weren't the simplest. So, let's consider as an alternative the phrase "Once upon a time …" from the perspective of an exclusively oral culture that lacks the opportunity or luxury of writing things down. How in that circumstance—which is to say, without numbers, without a capacity to codify dates, months, years, let alone decades and centuries—would one measure the past? Even more, how would one differentiate the more immediate past (one's childhood, say) from the more remote past (one's grandmother's childhood), but also necessarily from the ancient past (one's tribe's or even one's gods' origins)? What can these past*s*—immediate, remote, *and* ancient—even mean when they must all be housed together simultaneously in one's head? When exactly is *when* when there are no specific ways to delineate that point by way of a diary, calendar, or history timeline? How are we then to know and keep in orderly mind that the French Revolution came before Charles de Gaulle, but after the Renaissance? Or that Buddha appeared in the fifth century BCE, and Mohammed, some one thousand years later, in the sixth century CE?

We'll come back to how an oral way of knowing impacts the presentation and phenomenological experience of time in narrative (it is simply too pervasive and integral to be pulled apart here in a single go). For now, let us weigh in at least on the narrative and phenomenological reasons for "Once upon a time …." Perhaps a story will illustrate the concept most fruitfully— and with colorfully personal flair, to boot, as I turn once again to my own Punjabi grandmother to help us navigate a way of knowing with which many of us have lost semantic connection. (Again, that's why it's always helpful to study or take into account how preliterate children similarly, though obviously much less sophisticatedly, articulate, envision, and even package the past.) Here, I'll pull directly from a previous book, *The Sacred and the Cinema*, in which I argue that experiences of the sacred, of something as holy or divine, need to be understood in light of how orality and alphabetic literacy can impact the particularities of an individual's navigation of religion and the world of the gods. But the following story has far more to do with our current theme, much as its opening word suggests:

> Once, my grandmother was recounting for my sister the story of Krishna and the female cow-herders (*gopis*) smitten

with his flute playing. My sister, who was visiting [India] from Canada, had just completed a university religion course in which she had been introduced to the concept of cyclical time. As a test of my grandmother's personal means of comprehending time, my sister, after having been regaled with the story, asked *when* this encounter with the *gopis* had occurred. "Long ago," our grandmother responded.

"Yes, but *when*?" she inquired with a conscious attempt to nettle. "How long ago? When *exactly*?"

My grandmother was baffled. "What do you mean 'when'?" she brusquely replied. She became downright impatient, huffing at my sister's impolite importuning—and at what, in her mind, must have seemed an altogether absurd question. No doubt, too, she felt dispirited at not being able to accommodate a granddaughter's desire. But for my grandmother, "long ago," "before," and "in the past" were temporally satisfactory responses—if not the only ways to engage meaningfully with the past. "When *exactly*?" as it applies to the past implies a written record of history, one through which dates can be verified and time linearized. Without writing, history in the modern sense cannot exist, and so time must defer to the hazy durational telescoping that circumscribes much myth.[1]

In other words, "Once upon a time …" pays inadvertent tribute to the amalgamated nature of oral *past*-time (as distinct from a mere pastime). When conceived by someone like my grandmother who was fundamentally oral—but no less by my college students when recounting, in somewhat unconsciously rote fashion, a fairy tale or fable from their youth—what that stock phrase really implies is, *At some point before us—which is to say, during a time that, due to oral circumstance, we can only really demarcate as either "recently" or "long ago"—something happened, and it was important enough for our learning, well-being, religiosity, or communal survival for me to be recounting it to you now* … For those who yearn for a specific example drawn from an actual narrative, how about the following opening of the Norse epic *The Saga of the*

Volsungs: "Here we begin by telling of a man who was named Sigi, and it was said that he was the son of [the god of war] Odin."[2] However amorphous the past to which this story is traveling back may be, it is doing so because the story needs to be—warrants being—extended *into the future.*

Today, if we want narratively to strike a tone that is mythic (or, more likely, satirically stereotypic), we might consider beginning a story this way. But "Once upon a time ..." is so much more than merely the means for creating the semblance or illusion of myth. In fact, "long ago" and "once upon a time," it was the only way conceivable to project or conjure a past clouded in preliterate obscurity. No wonder that so many children, when they hear that beginning, settle in eagerly and easily with the expectation that they will be transported to a time and place lacking in historical definition, one mystically primordial as the necessarily conflated oral past is.

Notes

1 Nayar, *Sacred and the Cinema*, 4.
2 *Saga of the Volsungs*, 35.

References

Nayar, Sheila J. *The Sacred and the Cinema: Reconfiguring the Genuinely Religious Film*. New York: Bloomsbury, 2009.

The Saga of the Volsungs: The Norse Epic of Sigurd the Dragon Slayer. Trans. Jesse L. Byock. New York: Penguin Books, 1990.

8 A digression on the "once upon a time..." of *Star Wars*

Perhaps no contemporary text better wields "Once upon a time ..." as a means dynamically of fusing the past with the future than the *Star Wars* movie franchise. Each of its ten films begins, after all, with the words, "A long time ago in a galaxy far, far away ..." In this way, *Star Wars* prepares its audience to anticipate a science-fiction future that will nonetheless abide by, or that conceives itself as fully embedded in, a narrative form that stretches back to storytelling in its most ancient form: *myth*. Or, if we prefer kindred terms that likewise conjure oral ways knowing, we might resort to *epic,* or *saga*. (Indeed, the opening-crawl motif that the *Star Wars* films share likewise sutures the discrete movies together like a saga.) I don't say all this conjecturally either. It's fairly well known that George Lucas made concrete use in developing the original *Star Wars* of Joseph Campbell's books on comparative mythology, particularly his *The Hero with a Thousand Faces*. (Lucas even called Campbell "my Yoda.") Campbell's intentions were somewhat Jungian; that is, he wanted to shine a light on those archetypal persons or patterns that appeared *across* ancient cultures, both eastern and western: the Hero who is called to some necessary adventure, for instance; the Mentor who helps train him; the Trickster who tries to disrupt the hero's noble goals; and the final Life-Death Ordeal, to which the hero must submit.

But what *Before Literature* will argue, and in fact illustrate at every turn, is that many of these archetypes endure not because—or, at least, not purely because—of some original "monomyth" that binds us at our deepest core as a single, united humanity. Rather, it's because such archetypes are the most *economical* means by which to package a story that has to be carried through the generations without the assistance of writing— which is to say, by way almost exclusively of mind, tongue, and ear. In other words, many of the features that characterize "myth" are not merely reflective of some inherently theological worldview or derived from deep ego-consciousness (as wrested from Carl Jung's theories on the human psyche); they are also the means by which oral stories *had* to be delivered in order for them to be successfully passed on. (Recall Chapter 4, "The myth and the mythical, the epic and the epical.") We might argue, in fact, that the *Star Wars* franchise succeeds with all ages, with children no less than adults, precisely because of its reliance on our more natural—which is to say, more oral—ways of engaging with story.

To be sure, each *Star Wars* film's opening deployment of that ancient stock phrase occurs in writing: the verbal tag scrolls or crawls upward across the screen as inscription, as text, perhaps intentionally harkening back to the biblical film epics of the 1950s and, certainly, based on Lucas' own telling, on the episodic film series *Flash Gordon*. Here, then, is a perfect example of how, even in cultures that are now built on a literate architecture—street signs, databases, laws and policies in triplicate, how-to books— oral characteristics can continue to be put into playful or pedagogical interplay with the written word. (We'll be visiting some other examples of this later on.) Indeed, precisely because of this interplay, I feel the need to reassert that these oral ways of negotiating story are not inferior, primitive, or second-rate, certainly not when in a context unadulterated by inscription. Rather, the distinct means by which a narrative must be communicated and transmitted in an oral milieu calls for an entirely different but no less sophisticated set of norms. You're certainly free to disagree with me on this, oh, you readers who may be too entrenched in your alphabetically literate means of negotiating the world; but I'm going to ask that you wait until the end of this book before you contact me via Twitter to lodge your disagreement!

What I really want to foreground, moreover, is the way the *Star Wars* series ingeniously binds the past, present, and (our potential) future through that simple, but certainly not simplistic, recurrent opening of "A long time ago in a galaxy far, far away ...." We are immediately made closer to the story through that distance, however paradoxical that may sound, just as the very indeterminacy or uncertainness of our cinematic time and place magically manages both to estrange the story *and* to render it our own. In a sense, we are being told that the *when* and the *where* of the story are much less recoupable or important than our ownership of the *what*.

Perhaps, then, it's not so much that a story like *Star Wars* doesn't have a definitive beginning (as per the last chapter's title). More accurate might be to say that "Once upon a time ..." indicates a beginning that begins—without any self-consciousness—entirely in the middle of things.

9   Beginning *in medias res*

As we've addressed to some degree already, time is or, rather, cannot be completely linear in the oral milieu. That does not preclude the recognition that human life follows a relatively unbendable trajectory, from infant, to youth, to adult, to elder; or that one event happens before another. But because oral cultures are not able to track these numerically—to configure, for example, that 11,000 BCE precedes the nineteenth century CE, which itself precedes the years 1215 and 1812—how can a story ever really have a beginning that is lodged definitively and tangibly in historically situated time? Indeed, the relative incapacity of pinning time down may be one of the reasons that an oral bard like Homer began his epical recounting entirely *in media res*, which is the Latin way of saying that he narratively thrust his listeners straight "into the middle of things." In the case of the *Iliad*, for instance, we don't begin "at the beginning" of the decade-long Achaean siege of Troy. Nor are we provided any sort of time-date-place preamble or helpful placement-related exposition, let alone any setup of "Once upon a time, a baby called Achilles was born …" Rather, we are plunked right into the middle of a feud between Achilles and his Trojan enemies. Even more, we are thrust at once into a *mood*:

> Rage—Goddess, sing the rage of Peleus' son Achilles,
> murderous, doomed, that cost the Achaeans countless losses,
> hurling down to the House of Death so many sturdy souls,
> great fighters' souls, but made their bodies carrion,

feasts for the dogs and birds,
and the will of Zeus was moving toward its end.
Begin, Muse, when the two first broke and clashed,
Agamemnon lord of men and brilliant Achilles.
What god drove them to fight with such a fury?
Apollo the son of Zeus and Leto. Incensed at the king
he swept a fatal plague through the army—men were dying
and all because Agamemnon spurned Apollo's priest.
Yes, Chryses approached the Achaeans' fast ships
to win his daughter back, bringing a priceless ransom
and bearing high in hand, wound on a golden staff,
the wreaths of the god, the distant deadly Archer.[1]

And so, Homer sets the stage for our (or rather, his) narrative nosedive into the exigencies of Achilles' quarrel with the king Agamemnon. As for the origins of their quarrel, that we will have to wait for—both in terms of when it is presented in the *Iliad* and also when we will discuss it here.

Suffice it to say for now that, according to Walter J. Ong, launching into a story *in medias res* may have been the only natural way for an oral poet like Homer to approach a lengthy narrative—especially a narrative that Homer was mentally plucking from his larger internal storage drive of stories having to do with the Trojan War. Or, to borrow from Horace writing in *Ars poetica* (*The Art of Poetry*, ca. 13 BCE)—the concept of *in medias res* originates with him—that ideal epic poet does not start the story of the Trojan War "from the egg," which is to say, with the birth of Helen of Troy; instead, Homer "always hurries on to the outcome and snatches his listener into the very middle of things—just as if they were already known."[2] (Note how Horace identifies Homer's audience as a group of listeners, not readers.)

When the ancient Roman poet Virgil penned his epic the *Aeneid* from around 29 to 16 BCE, he, too, would begin *in medias res*, though his was a concerted act of imitation. If his epic begins with a divinely inspired storm that blows its hero, Aeneas, off his intended course, that's because Virgil was emulating ancient

Greek poetry—Homer's *Odyssey*, and later *Iliad*, particularly. Virgil's choice of opening, in other words, was not the consequence of his having to remember, organize, and transmit story exclusively by way of memory. No, for him, Homer's works now existed *in writing*; and, so, Virgil could use them not only as a guide and inspiration (Aeneas makes an appearance in the *Iliad*), but also as the "original" epics to which he could tether his own, entirely fabricated national epic of Rome's founding. This is also why one can find, as early as in Plato (d. ca. 348 BCE), oral bards being denigrated for their allegedly artless skills. Why? Because all they did now was repeat, in uncreative and stultifying fashion, memorized lines from the works of long-gone bards like Homer. Though certainly Virgil was culturally and temporally closer to the universe of orality than we are, ultimately his *Aeneid* qualifies as what literary scholars sometimes refer to as a *secondary epic*: an epic that is epical in style and structure because it consciously models itself on an initially oral or *primary epic*. While, today, some of us may think of Homer as coextant creatively with Virgil, the two are in fact radically different in terms of their motivations.

What's no less intriguing is that these same sorts of *in-medias-res* openings can be found in modern stories—and here I don't mean merely stories intentionally mimicking the epics of yore. Consider, for instance, the superhit Bollywood formula films from the 1970s to the 1990s, whose audiences rarely had any exposure to Homer, and even less likely to Virgil or Horace. In films from this period, spectators are consistently plunged, often with shocking abruptness, into a story already underway. Sometimes this occurs by way of an exploit or conversation already in progress, or a friendship being made, or even lightning ominously striking amidst reverberating thunder as a child runs through the streets in desperate search of aid. No silent lead-ups or slow establishing shots here. Why? Very possibly because these latter openings—noiseless, inert—are tied to the *eye* more so than to the *voice*. Their emphasis is on presenting information that privileges the act of looking, not hearing. (Even silent films from the early twentieth century began with live or recorded music that came before—that even augured—the arrival of the visuals.)

True, one might contend that the films' Indian audiences were culturally anticipating a beginning akin to that found in a familiar epic like the *Mahabharata*, with its equally swift plunge *in medias res* into a story of cousins at arms. And this notwithstanding that Hindu epic, as it exists today, has been massively thickened by additions made to the original story. (This is yet another fascinating way by which originally oral and subsequently literate texts experience mixes and mergers through time.) That such *in-medias-res* openings span oral epics across disparate cultures, however, as well as across disparate time periods, suggests that a more persuasive origin for their structural similarities might have to do with the way the stories had to be told. Again, it wasn't merely for stylistic or dramatic reasons that Homer wanted to begin with a sense of urgency, but because, when it comes to long narrative poems for which the poet is pulling from an even greater store of related events, this may be the only imaginable way to begin. What's more, because any discrete performance of an oral epic is always part and parcel of a *preknown* story—of a story that is neither new nor concocted but already communally shared and being carried forward through time—that epic is always, in a manner of speaking, already in progress!

Notes

1 Homer, *Iliad*, 77.
2 This particular translation of the Latin original (ll. 147–149) comes from Laird, *Powers of Expression*, 159 n. 17.

References

Homer. *The Iliad*. Trans. Robert Fagles. New York: Penguin Classics, 1998.

Laird, Andrew. *Powers of Expression, Expressions of Power: Speech Presentation and Latin Literature*. Oxford: Oxford University Press, 1999.

10 Ending anti-*in medias res*— and pro-status quo

Ever notice how movies critically classified as "art films" often conclude, much like modern literary novels do, in ways that are entirely ambiguous and irresolute? That is, as spectators or readers, we are denied knowing just *how* their stories really end— whether happily or doomed; whether the girl gets the boy or not; whether or not that protagonist whom we just followed for so many hours (or pages) even survived. In a sense, these sorts of stories end in the way that oral epics typically begin: in a manner that feels incomplete or ongoing; in a kind of limbo; basically *in medias res*!

The common scholarly adage is that art films end in the middle of things because they want to keep us thinking beyond our actual engagement with the text. Our immersion in the story is intended to extend past the theater where we've screened the film (or the days spent materially absorbed in the novel). Either that, or these stories are attempting, more philosophically, to reflect the un-finished-ness of life. They don't "end" because no end is ever really an end, as the only real end is the one that comes with death. So, instead of finitude at a plot's denouement, what we get is fluidity, uncertainty, and, more optimistically sometimes, possibility.

When it comes to texts that are predominantly orally inflected, they virtually never resolve in this paradoxically open-ended way. Rarely are more questions than answers planted in our minds, and seldom, if ever, is our sense of not knowing heightened in lieu of our being provided a tidy tying-up of the plot. No, narratives that inhabit the epistemically oral realm are almost uniformly brought to a finite close. Consider, for instance, the two fairy tales I cited earlier with respect to their "Once-upon-a-time" openings: "Little Red Riding Hood" and "Goldilocks and the Three Bears." Very likely, you are familiar with their endings. The resolution of "Little Red Riding Hood" goes something like this:

> But then came a hunter, and he killed the wolf with an axe, and out of his body appeared Little Red Riding Hood and her grandmother. Then, all three filled the wolf's body with stones, and they sank it in the river. The end.

As for "Goldilocks and the Three Bears," perhaps you remember how "… the Three Bears saw Goldilocks sleeping in the Little Bear's bed, and, then she woke up, and she screamed, and ran away. The end." We may carry away with us a moral, a sense of relief or, at the least, a sense of conflict resolved, but we certainly don't carry away a story only half-told. (By the way, the original version of Goldilocks' story—before it got sanitized and eventually downgraded to a decorous "children's story" in print—was far clearer in its being in the anthropomorphized bears' camp, with Goldilocks even presented as a "little old woman.")

Even though the *Iliad* may be only the middle portion of Homer's larger canvas of stories of the Trojan War, the epic ends fairly definitively, with an Achaean feast and a Trojan funeral. And while in the Sumerian *Epic of Gilgamesh*, Gilgamesh may lose the plant of immortality on his journey home from the Underworld, he will nonetheless return to rule his kingdom nobly and wisely for many years. If we were to articulate in more philosophical terms the reasons for these finales being so resolute, we might put it this way: The oral epic can never terminate in suspension because such a suspension, rather than certifying our existence as a group, would put us, as a tribe, in a jeopardized state. Recall that, in the oral milieu, there is no such thing as a story that, for the sake of its perpetuation, doesn't require at least two parties, a teller and a listener. An ending that is ambiguous and uncertain would endanger that relationship, as it would, too, the cohesion of the group. Why? Because how, in a world where the word is ephemeral, can we afford a story that is intentionally incomplete—*not* spoken, *not* told.

One other salient reason for this requisite closure is, perhaps, most succinctly articulated by the classicist Eric Havelock. As he notes specific to the "Homeric state of mind," it is a "general state of mind"[1]—which is to say, a mind that reflects not the thinking of an individual, but of a collective (one's tribe, one's community, or, in the decidedly modern context, one's nation-state). As a result, its thinking, narratively speaking, is also of the sort that typically represents and reinforces the "general" and accordingly, wants to end in communal equilibrium, with the way things are now certified, with the status quo intact. Otherwise, there *is* no continuity of the group. So, oral epic must be inclined toward the protection and conservation of the existing social structure— which is precisely, why its heroes are ultimately bent toward physically and intellectually preserving the ordered society. Our *we*-ness depends on it.

Consider the traditional African oral poets known as *griots*, who, while highlighting and sometimes even reveling in episodes of disorder, always do so with an eye on the end game, where traditional order will be restored.[2] (That in past ages these raconteurs were typically attached to royal courts would have also indisputably predisposed them toward capitulation to the status quo.[3]) Any desires, beliefs, and especially insubordinate yearnings of the individual are, in these circumstances, embedded in the plural— in community and, so, in the stability of that community. The Mali *Epic of Sundiata*, for example, ends with Sundiata becoming king of an empire that he will guide toward greatness. If not, what would that spell for the oral community to whom his story belongs? An ending that doesn't suture the community together in effect denotes its collective demise! (I use the present tense intentionally here, as this epic, whose origins lie in the thirteenth century, is still recounted by griots today.) Is it any wonder, then, that only with literacy and print, as Marshall McLuhan advocates, do we get an "eager assertion of individual rights."[4] It's not that oral individuals don't have a sense of their own subjectivity or of themselves as discrete beings. Rather, it's that, in the formulation and sharing of narrative, they are inextricably bound to others through the voice-ear connection and, consequently, not prone to thinking of story as independently or privately experienced affairs.

So, while the *Epic of Sundiata* may share little culturally with the *Iliad*, that doesn't mean these two stories cannot, or do not, share underlying characteristics motivated by a primarily oral way of knowing—much as Michelangelo Antonioni's art film *L'avventura* shares its (ostensibly literately derived) open-endedness with a novel like James Joyce's *Portrait of the Artist as a Young Man*, in spite of their navigating very different cultural terrains.

But we need not pull exclusively from the past when it comes to this penchant for social restoration. How many Hollywood blockbuster movies can you think of that conclude without reinstating communal equilibrium? *Titanic*? *Avatar*? How about *Finding Nemo*, *Wall-E*, *Black Panther*, *Jurassic World*, even *The Dark Knight*? Defense of the status quo—an end that is "resolutionary" instead of revolutionary—is, in fact, one of the most persistent and durable characteristics of oral narrative to survive into the present day. Yes, there may be ten *Star Wars* movies, and while some of them may end with temporary cliffhangers, what is never unresolved, upset, or overturned is our certainty regarding the preeminence of which side reflects "our" ordered and order-desiring society. That is always narratively preserved in due course. So, when critics laud a novella such as Joseph Conrad's *Heart of Darkness* for its sophisticated refusal to end; for the way it simply breaks off in a way that foregrounds endings as "artificial, arbitrary"—this is the eminent literary scholar Peter Brooks speaking—as "minor rather than major chords, casual and textual rather than cosmic and definitive,"[5] we need to recognize the alphabetically literate reasons for *Heart of Darkness*'s capacity to do so.

It's not that people like Brooks, or me, or you ought to be blamed for having grown neurologically and expectantly into our literately inflected environment. But we do need to refrain from assuming that that environment is somehow "authentic" or "natural," when in fact it only feels that way due to habituation. Eventually, I'll even address why the epistemically oral realm might *rightfully* indulge in what Brooks described as the "artificial" and "cosmic." For now, though, let's continue unpacking the whats and whys of oral storytelling's structure.

Notes

1 Havelock, *Preface to Plato*, 135.
2 Diawara, "Oral Literature," 201.
3 Early in the history of writing, scribes, too, were often associated with royal houses.
4 McLuhan, *Gutenberg Galaxy*, 220.
5 Brooks, *Reading for the Plot*, 314.

References

Brooks, Peter. *Reading for the Plot: Design and Intention in Narrative.* Cambridge, MA: Harvard University Press, 1992.

Diawara, Manthia. "Oral Literature and African Film: Narratology in *Wend Kuuni*." *Questions of Third Cinema*. Eds. Jim Pines and Paul Willemen. London: BFI Publishing, 1989. 199–211.

Havelock, Eric. *Preface to Plato*. Cambridge, MA: The Belknap Press of Harvard University Press, 1963.

McLuhan, Marshall. *The Gutenberg Galaxy: The Making of Typographic Man*. Toronto: University of Toronto Press, 1962.

11 "And this happened ... and then this ... and then ..."

Let's go back to that student standing in front of my classroom—let's call her Lucy—thanks to her willingness publicly to recount a story from her youth. One of the first characteristics that I try to lure her audience into discerning, I do by way of un-contextualized gestures. That is, I stand next to Lucy and periodically raise a finger as she tells the story of Little Red Riding Hood. One—and then another—and then another of my fingers goes up, until finally I have to change hands in order to account for the seven, eight, nine times that Lucy has ... Done what? Like I said, I haven't told the students what I'm tallying. They have to figure it out for themselves, and eventually they always do. They realize that what I'm keeping count of is Lucy's repeated use of a single grammatical construction, the conjunction: those tiny little words that adjoin words to phrases, and independent clauses to other independent clauses. And Lucy's stringing her sentences together by way of a veritable litany of them:

> *But* then came a hunter, *and* he killed the wolf with an axe, *and* out of his body appeared Little Red Riding Hood and her grandmother. *Then*, all three filled the wolf's body with stones *and* they sank it in the river.

This, as Walter J. Ong reminds us, is a rhetorical style that is additive rather than subordinative[1]—with the former style stemming from oral delivery and the latter reflective of an inscriptive "tidying up" of those more conspicuously oral elements. You see, our natural inclination when talking *is* to string discrete thoughts together by way of conjunctions like "and," "but," and "then." But when we craft our speaking words on the page, we erase this episodic stringiness by subordinating some clauses to other, more major clauses. So, had Lucy jotted down precisely what she'd articulated above and shown it to her instructor of English composition, she probably would have been told to "refine" her wording, to "elevate" her written expression by tightening her prose. A more "writerly" version of her original narration might look something like this:

> When the hunter came, he killed the wolf with an axe. Upon Little Red Riding Hood and her grandmother appearing out of his body, all three filled the wolf's body with stones, eventually sinking it in the river.

But this sort of tightening—with its intentional elimination of the additive sequence "But ... and ... and ... Then ... and ..."— is hardly innate, let alone convenient, to someone who is orally recollecting a story. Subordination of this kind mandates being able to edit and rework the structure of sentences, which is something a lot easier done on the page than in one's head.

You can find that additive style reflected in the opening of the Hebrew Bible:

> In the beginning, God created the heaven and the earth. *Now* the earth was unformed and void ..., *and* darkness was ..., *and* the spirit of God. ... *And* God said. ... *And* there was light. *And* God saw the light ...; *and* God divided the light ..."[2]

This language is styled in a way that is practical for *listeners* to Genesis, as well as for the individual orally recounting the biblical creation story to them. In more modern versions of the Bible, these additive tendencies are often eliminated, with subordination put to syntactical use. The writers of the 1970 New American Bible, for instance, altered the sentence structure of the opening lines of Genesis in this way: "In the beginning, *when God created the heavens and the earth*, the earth was a formless wasteland …"[3] In later Bibles, in other words, the language is crafted, perhaps unwittingly, to appeal to those accustomed to reading (and modifying their own) words on the page.

The implication is, of course, that orally transmitted narratives cannot be structurally cohesive—tightly compact—in the way that alphabetic readers are trained to anticipate or favor. And this doesn't apply to storytelling on the level of the sentence alone. For the very same reasons, an oral narrative's entire plot, the order and intensity by which a story advances on the tongue of its bard—or even, potentially, across a movie screen—likewise lacks a compact tightness. (Just to clarify, *story* in the official argot of narratology, refers to the chronological order by which, as an example, the events of Achilles' life in the *Iliad* proceed; *plot*, quite distinctly, is the order by which those events are presented to us—given that Achilles' rage with Agamemnon comes before our ever learning what precipitated that rage.)

In fact, the very possibility of a "pyramidal plot"—one built on an ever-tightening rise in action and build of tension (a type we are so very accustomed to via Hollywood films)—is also a byproduct of a novel's or script's capacity to be written out and, hence, reorganized, modified, condensed, finessed, and so forth. Not unlike those modern Bible translators working diligently to tighten Genesis' sentences on the page, novelists and screenwriters can tighten with increasing intensity the *entire construction* of their stories. Some genres are especially driven by—are even the outright by product of—the more methodical and contrived ways of structuring a narrative that writing has induced. Mysteries and detective stories, for instance, require a careful "backward" knowledge of a story in order to drop clues and craft "relentlessly rising tension"[4]; and such intricately plotted sci-fi films such as Christopher Nolan's *Inception* and *Interstellar* could hardly exist without the technical assistance and creative liberties born of inscription.

Conversely—and in a kind of grander replication of the additive rhetorical style—the plots of lengthy oral narratives are *episodic.* Their scenes, their stories, their plots as a whole proceed in ways far less taut or tidily connected. Instead, they tend to pivot on thematic recurrences (for example, the war with Troy … followed by a lengthy altercation between the gods … and then back to the war …); on extended chronological breaks (Odysseus in the *Odyssey* enjoying a feast … followed by his really, really lengthy recounting of his travels/travails prior to reaching his current hosts' habitat …); as well as on a poet's taking shrewd advantage of the self-sufficient appeal of, say, a comic scene or one of heightened horror. (The latter was something identified with particular acumen by novelist and scholar of African epic Isidore Okpewho.[5])

Hopefully now you get the picture: that these narratives' actions and events are essentially sewn together, patch by patch. Indeed, this was something the ancient Greeks consciously understood about their own epic tradition, given that their term for it, *rhapsoidia*, literally meant a stitching together (from *rhaptein*, "to stitch," and *oide*, "ode or song").[6] Sometimes the stitching is so unabashedly explicit, as in the case of Icelandic sagas, that the modern reader may find the rhetorical style irksome, even intrusive: "Now there is this to be told … Now there is this to tell … Now there is this to be said …" In other words, this happened; and then this happened (which may have no bearing on what happened before); and then something else happened (maybe connected to the first this [or second this, or maybe not]); and so forth. Yes, this may undermine our contemporary zeal for causality (whereby this happened—which caused that to happen—which triggered the occurrences of one, two, and three more events). But in the oral-aural context, the episodic plot is far more comfortable, not to mention pragmatic: easier to follow, to digest, and also to narrate. Just try, for example, recounting exclusively by oral means the storyline of the film *Inception* or *Interstellar*!

Figure 11.1 A par (painting on cloth) depicting exploits central to the oral epic of the 14th-century Rajasthani folk hero-deity Pabuji (Pabuji Verteldoek [4669–1], Tropenmuseum). While this par dates from 1938, pars like it have long served as a visual accompaniment in ceremonies during which Pabuji's martial deeds are sung by priestly bards of the bhopa community. Prior to the performance, the par is unrolled to the blowing of conches, and incense and coconut are offered to the hero. The bard is then "assisted by his wife, his son (who may be an apprentice), or another person, who points to the scenes on the par about which he is singing."[7] There's apparently an intriguing gender discrepancy when it comes to who finds these stories engaging. Their heroic mode appeals "more to the men in the audience. In fact, women devotees of [Pabuji] tend to identify him with Krishna. Songs about [Pabuji] that women sing—outside the ritual of the par—may focus emotions on the baby Krishna."[8] Certainly this gives us pause to wonder: Does our academic privileging of the oral epics (with their traditionally masculinist emphasis) skew or restrict our more comprehensive understanding of any given culture?

Notes

1 Ong, *Orality and Literacy*, 37–39.
2 Genesis 1.1–3, *The Hebrew Bible*, a Hebrew-English Bible According to the Masoretic Text and the JPS 1917 Edition, retrieved from www.mechon-mamre.org/p/pt/pt0.htm. Emphases added.
3 Ong, *Orality and Literacy*, 37.
4 Ibid., 144.
5 Okpewho, *Epic in Africa*, 209–210.
6 Ong, "Oral Residue," 149.
7 "Par (paintings on cloth) from Rajasthan," *Kalarte.com*.
8 Ibid.

References

The Hebrew Bible, a Hebrew-English Bible According to the Masoretic Text and the JPS 1917 Edition. Retrieved July 28, 2107, from www.mechon-mamre.org/p/pt/pt0.htm.

Okpewho, Isidore. *The Epic in Africa: Toward a Poetics of the Oral Performance.* New York: Columbia University Press, 1979.

Ong, Walter J. *Orality and Literacy: The Technologizing of the Word.* London: Routledge, 1982.

———. "Oral Residue in Tudor Prose." *PMLA* 80, 3 (1965): 145–154.

"Par (paintings on cloth) from Rajasthan." *Kalarte.com*. Retrieved July 29, 2017, from http://kalarte.com/india/ra-c/ra-c1.html.

12 Epic examples of episodic epics

Because students in introductory literature courses are typically assigned *excerpts* from the oral epics, they are often not sufficiently exposed to the poems' highly episodic nature. Literary anthologies, which are often what instructors use—with the excerpts likely coming from Homer's *Iliad* or *Odyssey*—frequently include only the meatiest portions: parts carved out from what otherwise "drags" or diverts too far from the perceived major through-line of the story. The reasons for these anthologies doing so are relatively understandable. The epics, in their full form, are simply too long—and, yes, possibly too boring in parts to keep contemporary readers engaged (too many unfamiliar gods, too many foreign place-names, too many disjointed subplots and flights of poetic fancy). We, of course, have even less space in this book to give full account of their episodic structure. So, for the sake of expediency, let's consider just one, a heroic epic that is not only our most ancient, but also advantageously short, the *Epic of Gilgamesh*. It's a work, by the way, I think every individual ought to read, if for no other reason than to grasp just how fundamental and long-running our obsession with our own impermanence has been.

Gilgamesh fairly neatly cleaves as a narrative into two discrete parts. The first recounts the king Gilgamesh's encounters with the wild man, Enkidu. Gilgamesh, alas, is exceedingly rash and, so, at the behest of his own subjects, the goddess Ishtar creates Enkidu out of dust and water. Enkidu's job? To rival and, thus, mollify the king's ways. First, though, Enkidu needs to lose some of his own coarse, animalistic tendencies through an encounter with a prostitute; only then is he ready to take on Gilgamesh—although Gilgamesh, being our hero, ends up overcoming Enkidu in a wrestling match. Stripped overwhelmingly of his barbarism, Enkidu now joins Gilgamesh's city of Uruk, proceeding to become not only Gilgamesh's best friend but also his fellow adventurer. Together, they fell the Cedar Forest, killing its guardian Humbaba, after which they also slay the goddess Ishtar's Bull of Heaven, which she sent down to kill Gilgamesh for scorning her advances. (Note my careful *and* paradoxical attempt in this paragraph to employ a highly subordinative sentence structure, notwithstanding that my aim is to highlight the additive-episodic nature of an oral epic's plot structure!)

The second part of the narrative occurs after Enkidu's death, which Ishtar demanded as compensation for the loss of her bull. Distraught, Gilgamesh journeys to the Underworld, where he hopes to learn why humans must die and, if fortunate, to obtain the secret to immortality. While on his way home, he will lose the sacred plant that would have invested him with eternal living—a sea snake snatches it—Gilgamesh has at least been made privy during his time below to the story of the Great Flood, which was narrated to him by Utnapishtim, a former-day Noah from generations past (indeed, the flood story here is amazingly analogous to that in the Bible). But because Gilgamesh ultimately proves his mettle, particularly through bringing back the story of his experiences in the Underworld and building the great protective walls of Uruk, he rules a long time after, with his fame living on.

Now, were a feature film today to be made of this epic, whether animated or live-action, almost certainly its screenwriters would spend a good amount of time figuring out how more logically to bind *Gilgamesh*'s first half to its second. Probably they would rely, in terms of plot design, on something close to what some dramatists refer to as Freytag's Pyramid. Gustav Freytag developed this structural model based on his study of plays by the likes of Shakespeare and the ancient Greeks, and with some major stimulation from Aristotle's *Poetics*. Freytag's model—that "pyramidal plot" to which earlier I alluded—usually entails an *inciting incident,* which, while starting the action, generally comes only after the drama's *exposition,* which is to say, a provision of information that we need in order to follow the story.

So, let's say we start with the king Gilgamesh as a bored and restless man with no real opponents. Let's also make him an aging king, one whose most manly, muscular feats he fears are behind him and whose only progeny are daughters. He's lost interest in being a leader, in short. This exposition gives way to the inciting incident: Enkidu lured and bedded by a maiden disguised as a harlot at the behest of a queen of a nearby city, who—here I'm taking major Hollywoodish poetic license—wants to get back at Gilgamesh for having long ago spurned her. She will send Enkidu to Gilgamesh in order, insidiously, to lay claim to his empire. Thus begins the *ascending action,* with the comparatively young and virile Enkidu going on an attack of Uruk, before finally being beaten by Gilgamesh in extended hand-to-hand combat. Yes, Gilgamesh has won—but in part because Enkidu's youth has rejuvenated him. Thus does the ancient bromance begin. The action continues to build, the tension forever increasing—because, as their friendship is formed, and Humbaba is killed, and lands are conquered, that queen still has Enkidu under her thumb. But finally, Enkidu's loyalty to Gilgamesh overrides his loyalty to the queen, and so *she* leashes that Bull of Heaven to destroy Uruk, with *she* ultimately planning and executing Enkidu's death—to punish Gilgamesh.

When Gilgamesh then descends into the Underworld to learn of the Great Flood, what he discovers is how that queen, unbeknownst to her, has killed *her own son,* Enkidu—who also happens to be *Gilgamesh's son.* (Yes, I am shamelessly stealing here from Sophocles' *Oedipus Rex* because, although I once worked as a screenwriter myself, I was never a very good one.) So, of course, Gilgamesh wants now, more than ever, to find that plant (we'll make it a plant of restoration rather than immortality), given that now it's his *son,* the future ruler of Uruk, whom he wants to resuscitate. Consequently, the attempted acquisition of that medicinal plant becomes the most dynamic ascent toward the movie's *climactic point* (perhaps a string of fights with scorpions and crocodiles, before finally Gilgamesh retrieves the magic shrub—only, on his way back, to lose it in the fiercest combat with a giant snake. This brings about a *fall in action* (his return home empty-handed), leading to the film's finale, its *denouement* (recognition that his city walls, which his people are rebuilding, will give him and Enkidu a *real* immortality—because he will have their story baked into its bricks ... and also, as it turns out, because that maiden has had Enkidu's child—a son.

No such feature film has ever been made. And frankly, given my heavier reliance than even in the original epic on that old, dogged trope of Vindictive Female, I'm not sure I would want to see this one produced. Still, there is something odd that our oldest story—and a mortality-obsessed buddy story, at that—has never been adapted for the screen. By contrast, the Old English epic *Beowulf* has been adapted by Hollywood screenwriters more than several times in the last few decades. Perhaps the appeal is *Beowulf*'s proto-Western European origins (the story takes place in Scandinavia). Whatever the commercial motivations, *Beowulf*'s adaptors are always trying to strengthen the causal connections between its various episodes, which are no less disconnected than those of *Gilgamesh*.

For those unfamiliar with the original story of *Beowulf*: The cannibalistically vicious attacks of the monster Grendel on the Danes' great mead hall are finally brought to end by that tribe's heroic guest, the Geat warrior Beowulf—though not without his inciting the fury of Grendel's Mother, whom Beowulf must also eventually slay. Flash forward to decades later, with Beowulf, now an old man, returning to battle a gold-hoarding dragon. While Beowulf is himself annihilated, his younger companion succeeds in killing the beast. So, back now to Hollywood's methods of tightening and more intricately plotting this Anglo-Saxon story: These have included beefing up the monster Grendel's relationship to the human clan he attacks. Sometimes his mother is even made the past lover of the clan's king and Grendel their bastard son. When it comes to the epic's second part, Beowulf's encounter with the dragon at whose hands—or claws, rather—he dies: Often the screenwriters jettison that installment altogether or make the youth, who succeeds in slaughtering the dragon, Beowulf's son.

Could those causally incongruent parts—Grendel/Grendel's Mother/Beowulf and, later, Beowulf/Dragon—be the by product of a stitching together of independent stories about that hero (or maybe different heroes even, now conflated under a single name)? Yes, very possibly. Whether this would have happened during *Beowulf*'s exclusively oral existence or sometime after, as a consequence of being written down, I cannot say. Truth be told, so many of our earliest stories come without clear provenances or history of origins, let alone a convenient accounting of how "This part was taken from X …" and "This part was told by Y …" Indeed, the same might be attributable to stories in the *Odyssey*—that is, that some of Odysseus' adventures with various ogres or sirens began as folktales that were then organically embedded into Homer's sprawling epic. And in the case of Odysseus (not to mention, to lesser extents, both Beowulf and Gilgamesh), what better way to accommodate a series of unrelated and hence episodic encounters than by way of a hero who is taking a trip?

We know that the *Epic of Gilgamesh* was likely altered after its long-term migration through exclusively oral means—which is to say, before finally it got incised into clay tablets in that ancient Sumerian form of writing known today as cuneiform (from the Latin word *cunues*, meaning "wedge"). The key to this narrative accretion or adding-on is evident in the way the epic now opens. For, amidst the First Tablet's laudation of the city walls erected by Gilgamesh, we are informed that, upon his return from his journey to the Underworld, "He carved on a stone stela all of his toils …" In other words, possibly bookending the initially oral story of Gilgamesh—or, rather, the cumulative, strung-together stor*ies* of Gilgamesh—is mention of what could have only occurred after its inscription onto a material substance—a technological feat that, surely by no accident, is one for which Uruk is historically known.

13 [[Boxes] within boxes] within boxes

Although alphabetically literate cultures may train folks to read and write and, so, to *think* written stories, the stories they produce are no more creative or technically skilled than those of oral cultures. Just try recounting all the juggled pieces of an extended narrative like the *Odyssey* from your head! This prompts a very worthwhile question: In the latter circumstance, in the oral circumstance, how exactly *does* one keep all those pieces in play? Certainly, an episodic structure, which we covered, is one way. But did you notice how, in the stories I used to elucidate that characteristic, virtually all of them incorporated or made use of what we today call the *flashback*? This device allows for a non-sequential, retrospective inclusion of information or story that would be too complicated or impossible to incorporate into the principle storyline. Recall, for example, Utnapishtim's protracted account of his experience of the Great Flood to Gilgamesh; or Odysseus' protracted chronicling for his hosts of his earlier adventures while voyaging on the Mediterranean Sea.

Flashbacks, in these circumstances, serve a number of functions. They can allow for a recall of events that happened earlier in time or provide needed clarification, or they may feed their audience data necessary to elicit empathy, justification, or the like. In other words, these flashbacks are *not* intended to complicate the nature of narrative, such as is the case with respect to a work like Joseph Conrad's *Heart of Darkness*. That novella, which in many respects comprises flashbacks within one giant flashback, wants intentionally to trouble and consciously call into question the coherence and articulacy of any recollected story. Oral narratives, however, never employ flashbacks for such intellectual or philosophical purposes. Instead, they nest information in boxes in order to transmit story more neatly—like "nuts within shells," as Peter Brooks nicely describes;[1] or like a Chinese puzzle composed of boxes within boxes, as Cedric Whitman aptly discerned of the *Iliad's* structure.[2] In the case of the *Mahabharata*, more specifically, we have an inside box comprising a sage who is recounting the story of King Nala to the Pandava princes, with those princes also inhabiting an outer box—because their story is being recounted by a later sage to their own great-grandsons. But this is not a structural puzzle meant to mess with your mind, as in the case of *Heart of Darkness* or a film like *Inception*. No, this is a structuring method intended to keep your mind—and the various strands of the story—on a decipherable and apprehensible track.

Keep in mind, too, that in the context of oral narrative, often these flashbacks are really, really—*really*—extensive in length, such as, again, when Gilgamesh listens to the timeworn Story of the Flood, or Odysseus regales the Phaeacians with the particulars of his past seafaring adventures. In fact, Odysseus' dinnertime story constitutes a whopping sixth of the entire *Odyssey*. Often these stories-within-the-story are so long in duration that I suspect no producer or editor today would be keen to foreground their presence in a contemporary adaptation, for fear of their overtaking the principal storyline and, thus, diminishing its magnetic thrust.

So, why can these flashbacks—why *would* these flashbacks—be so lengthy in oral storytelling? Even more broadly, why would flashbacks be such an essential and relatively universal component of the structure of oral epic? Whether you consider the oral traditions of ancient Sumer, ancient Greece, or ancient India; or the songs of those bards of the former Yugoslavia, whom Milman Parry recorded in the 1930s; or that fourteenth-century folk epic of Pabuji still performed today in Rajasthan—flashbacks to past times predominate.

We could argue that the omnipresence of these flashbacks, including the long, drawn-out ones, was simply a case of listeners not expecting or desiring a strict linear progression of events; of their not feeling particularly uneasy about frequent interruptions to any principle storyline. Perhaps not unlike the king in *1001 Arabian Nights* who has to wait every night for a new story (within a story)—because his tale-telling wife Scheherazade is trying to delay his killing her—listeners would have had to wait until the following evening for the commencement of that "past" story to begin. In this way, there may have been an actual temporal pause, a delay in the telling that comfortably demarcated and separated the narrative present from the past.

Today, we may ignore or underestimate the integral nature of these structural hiatuses, given that we're no longer beholden to a bard whose recounting of his narrative might stretch for days. We now have the capacity to continue reading an epic (or to stop reading one *in media res*) whenever and wherever we like, whether by free will, or whim, or because we have a 10:30 appointment. Our experience of story has been wrested from its lodging in an actual, material human teller. Instead, we engage with a story as if it were something autonomous. We conceive of narratives as possessing lives of their own—even when we're engaging with them aurally in the form of audio books.

The fairly definitive lines in the oral milieu between a story's "past" and "present" (why I've put these in quotes will eventually become clear) are of consequence for another reason. Often, with the aid of a single question, my students swiftly determine the reason for themselves. So that you, too, can one-up me, here's the question: "What about when something relatively *recent* happens that merits being carried into the future—a great war perhaps, or a natural disaster, or a queen kidnapped by the evil king of an enemy nation, or the defeat (finally!) of a sea serpent that was capsizing canoes?"

In other words, once upon a time, the story of the Great Flood probably was a discrete and independent oral narrative told by the Sumerian people. But when Gilgamesh's story was deemed significant enough for the telling; when *it* became the principle narrative—whether by intent or accident—that diluvian tale from the now-distant past was conveniently and conservatively encased in a box. "Utnapishtim's Story of the Great Flood," let's call it, was now placed into the larger box of Gilgamesh's "Journey to the Underworld." Of course, a possible repercussion in the privileging of newer story—or of more recent memories, we should probably say—is that parts of the past would require sloughing off. And if parts needed willfully to be forgotten, what better to shave away than memories that no longer seemed germane or consequential to the extant group? Alternatively, events or personages from the more distant past that warranted survival might be economically compressed with those from the less distant past. After all, neither of these pasts was measurably bound or historically fixed and situated. Consider, for instance, the thirteenth-century Icelandic *Saga of the Volsungs*, in which characters are presented as existing concurrently, when in fact they lived decades and, sometimes even, centuries apart. The same is believed to be the case of the dozens of warriors in the *Iliad*.

How precisely this happened and over what length of time, I can hardly say, especially since some of what I'm suggesting here can only ever be conjecture. Unlike computer-generated drafts of a story or the updated editions of a novel, oral epics leave far fewer traces regarding how they've been altered, edited, enriched, or condensed through time. Nevertheless, the preponderance of these boxed events within the predominant storyline of any lengthy poem—no matter whether that poem is ancient Indian, or ancient Greek, or ancient Aboriginal—suggests that the flashback is simply too integral a part of oral storytelling not to have been the most efficacious means of preserving older pasts within more recent pasts.

Of course, those more recent pasts, to reprise, are always, in the oral ecology, being presented *in the present*. That is, an event like Beowulf's nailing of Grendel's amputated arm to the lintel of the mead hall was always being told by a poet who existed in space-time alongside and with those who were digesting his story. While today we may pick up Dostoevsky or Dickens, Plato's *Republic* or Edward Gibbon's *The History of the Decline and*

Fall of the Roman Empire—or even *Beowulf*—and engage with ideas from the past that have been preserved, that is impossible in a fundamentally oral environment. In the latter scenario, history is not something detachedly past, but something always carried in and part of the present, odd as that may sound to our contemporary ears. In other words, Dostoevsky's *Crime and Punishment* or Dickens' *Oliver Twist* would only exist were it integrated *into* the poet's present-day songs.

As a result, it's very likely that what would get sloughed off through time were events that no longer spoke to the contemporary group's cultural values. This is something that the anthropologist Jack Goody was key in detecting—as was, too, Claude Levi-Strauss when proposing that a group does not contest its own myths, but instead transforms them while believing all the while that they are actually repeating them.[3] Inevitable, in other words—and perhaps unnervingly for us today—is that what gets transmitted, including those past events deemed worthy of preservation, gets *recreated* along the way. Hector, for instance—that Trojan prince who will ultimately succumb to Achilles' rage—conceivably had a memorialized existence before he got amalgamated with other figures into that greatest warrior of Troy.

As was discovered in the late twentieth century by way of the Tiv of southeastern Nigeria, inconvenient truths could be conveniently buried or discarded, even in the case of genealogies.[4] And why not? The Tiv, after all, were keeping their records orally—and, so, current political circumstances were far more vital than what might have happened generations ago. Besides, since our brains die with us, in the oral context, all the information stored in those organs would be communally erased in less than a century. So, while written versions of the Tiv people's genealogies—as kept by their British colonizers at the time— might have pointed to discrepancies between what the Tiv had said 40 years prior and what they were presently claiming, what mattered to them were hardly some "idle" historical accuracies about their forebears. Nor could these accuracies necessarily comprise "truth." What mattered, what was critical, was what relations were *now*—and, so, best to alter the Tiv family tree in favor of, say, a recent leader's rise in social relations.

Notes

1 Brooks, *Reading for the Plot*, 256.
2 Ong, *Orality and Literacy*, 27.
3 Lévi-Strauss, *Naked Man*, 655.
4 Goody and Watt, "Consequences of Literacy," 33–34.

References

Brooks, Peter. *Reading for the Plot: Design and Intention in Narrative.* Cambridge, MA: Harvard University Press, 1992.

Goody, Jack, and Ian Watt. "The Consequences of Literacy." *Literacy in Traditional Societies.* Ed. Jack Goody. Cambridge: Cambridge University Press, 1968. 27–68.

Lévi-Strauss, Claude. *The Naked Man (Mythologiques,* Vol. 4). Trans. John and Doreen Weightman. Chicago: University of Chicago Press, 1990.

Ong, Walter J. *Orality and Literacy: The Technologizing of the Word.* London: Methuen, 1982.

14 Flashbacks, masala style

So, here's something fascinating: That propensity toward flashbacks which is characteristic of oral epic was also a mainstay in hit Bollywood films from the 1970s to the 1990s. So, too, were stand-alone sketches and narrative deviations, often slapstick or violent in nature, which likewise amplified the movies' already-episodic feel. For those of you who are shrewdly wondering if I may be overstating the case, listen to how film scholars K. Moti Gokulsing and Wimal Dissanayake describe the typical Hindi film storyline in their 1998 book *Indian Popular Cinema*: Said storyline, they propose, "does not progress in a linear fashion but meanders, with detours and stories within stories," in a "circular form of narration [that] is commonly found in classical and folk literature."[1] Much like the *Mahabharata* and the *Odyssey*, in other words, these movies, too, were assembled like a Chinese puzzle with its boxes within boxes.

Of course, when it comes to a commercial industry like Bollywood, we need also ask, as critics often did, if financial incentives might have motivated the films' piecemeal assemblage. That is, did loosely strung-together plotlines make an overarching story more comfortable, easier to follow, and less complicated to digest—or was this instead an expedient way of producing cheap movies? After all, a haphazardly strung-together sequence of events—fights, cabaret shows, stereotyped stars flexing their muscles—required little forethought when it came to devising storylines. On the other hand, couldn't we argue that discontinuous structure more honestly and accurately mirrors human existence? If our lives proceed as tightly structured "plot," they do so only in the briefest blips (with very few of us running in relentlessly ascending action toward our life's climactic point). Episodic structure, in other words, makes space for the sorts of horrific, humorous, and celebratory incidents that punctuate our lives and that often feel autonomous (a parent's death, a child's birth, that glorious first day on the job, that traumatic night when you were assaulted). In the case of 1970s–1990s Bollywood, no digressions were more consistently crafted for their freestanding appeal than song-and-dance numbers. And because these musical interludes are often set against the backdrop of a wedding, engagement ceremony, or religious festival, they function much like the endless succession of formal events that appear in the oral epics. As for why this would be: That's because ceremonious occasions like marriages and funerals repeat and reinforce tribal existence[2]; they emphasize social unity and the predominance of the group.

But let's return to my earlier acknowledgement that this late-twentieth-century tendency in Bollywood toward ragged, disjointed filmmaking—toward the additive rather than the subordinative—might have been due less to audience expectations than to industry profiteering. Indeed, film critics often contended that the inclusion of musical numbers hindered cinematic self-expression. How could directors ever hope to project an onscreen world that reflected reality when they had to include at least a half-dozen song-and-dance numbers? One of the inevitable byproducts of those numbers, moreover, was that the films were forced into being episodic rather than tightly woven. It's worth our wondering, though, whether the expectation of this particular economy of storytelling—indeed, the audience's general *affinity* for it—meant that the motivations went deeper than some Machiavellian opportunism on the part of movie moguls. In fact, the films' regular deployment of the flashback provides us in part the clue that their episodic structure may have had more to do with the oral derivation of the masala formula than with that formula's profitability for producers.

Flashbacks, you see, are persistent and unremitting in these films, whether in the form of a hero nostalgically recollecting the travails of his protective mother, as in the film *Baazigar* (Trickster, 1993), or of a hero's mother recounting her grown son's adolescent descent into crime, as in *Khal Nayak* (Villain, 1993) (and for an hour of screen time in a three-hour film, no less!). In one of the most famous blockbusters in Indian film history, *Sholay* (Flames, 1975), we are made privy through flashback to how a police chief met the two thieves whom he now plans to hire to execute vengeance on behalf of his family. Not long after, we flash back for a protracted look at his family's idyllic past—followed by its tragic ruination, which includes the murder of his grandchildren at the hand of the man he now wants those thieves to slay. By the way, these sorts of present-past-present configurations continue to flourish in many a twenty-first-century superhit.

To be sure, what may be pleasurable in these moves back in time, as critics have mentioned, is a certain unofficial or secret history that is brought to the fore. But just as integral, I would suggest, is their concession to the importance of memory—and memory presented, more often than not, in ways that are intergenerational: a mother's reflections about her son, or a son's about his mother, or a patriarch revealing the story of their household's misfortune to his two grandsons, who will then go on to seek retribution. Why might this matter? Because what these sequential moves cement is the notion of family persisting *through time*. The dynastic lineage or blood clan is represented as something of a pre historical unit—which is to say, one that unites the past to the present through the explicitly spoken word. In oral cultures, it is only through this telling-listening transmission that the past is kept alive. Imagine how different, then, your experience would be had you been an Anglo-Saxon listening to *Beowulf*. That oral poem wouldn't merely be the story of a badass warrior named Beowulf. Rather, it would be *your* Beowulf and *your* story being told. Yes, readers today may well find that epic riveting still, but you, as that Anglo-Saxon of yore, would have been traveling in the footsteps of your totem ancestors. (As for why I say *totem*, we'll come back to that later.)

Hollywood storytelling also often acknowledges and avails itself of the power inherent in traveling back in time through word of mouth. Consider the film *Titanic* (1997), which is 90 percent in flashback. In case you've forgotten, the elderly Rose orally recounts the story of her brief but intense romance with the impoverished Jack on that ship doomed to sink in 1912. Why the inclusion of this framing device? According to film scholar Vivian Sobchack, the frame-tale of Rose recollecting the past operates as a kind of "hermetic shelter" that provides spectators an experience of authentic history filtered through bathos, through sentimentality and melodrama.[3] But we could just as well argue that, as a narrative return to earlier events, Rose's oral recounting conjures a sense of community and, better yet, continuity between the generations. Hence *this time* is linked to *that time*, such that who we are now is both orally and aurally sutured to what we have been. The aged Rose thereby serves as a kind of bard who is going to dramatize the particulars of that calamitous sinking of the *Titanic*.

Of course, Rose is a very upscale bard from a very upscale community. Nevertheless, even that, as we shall later see, may owe something to oral inflection—as might also that bathos to which Sobchack refers. In fact, I should probably point out at this juncture that any characteristic of the oral episteme on its own and isolated from the epistemic whole—whether episodic structure, or flashbacks, or melodrama—can be played with in ways that do not necessarily result in a film more orally than literately inflected. When it comes to the oral episteme of narrative, we're talking, quite crucially, about a *reticulate* set of attributes. And if you stick with reading this book, you'll see that I am indeed trying to persuade you that James Cameron's *Titanic* fits the bill of a film highly inflected by orality. That's probably also what made it such a worldwide blockbuster, including in India, Japan, Brazil, and even, in bootlegged form, in Afghanistan, where the literacy rate today is a mere 28 percent.

Not insignificantly, *Titanic* is also a narrative whose end (the calamitous sinking) we, as spectators, *already know*, much as would have been the case for an ancient oral poet's listeners.

The oral epics weren't mysteries, after all, but stories that, as collective wisdom, were told and retold throughout one's life. Thus even *Titanic*, we might argue, preserves that "curvature of time" which philosopher and cultural ecologist David Abram says is emblematic of oral cultures. Like those cultures, the film resists the learned linearity of the printed line, engaging instead with "a world of cycles within cycles within cycles."[4] And although there may have been only one Rose in the film, just think how many generations of "Homers" there must have been in operation before finally "our" Homer's story got written down.

Often scholars read these inter-generational and cyclical moves in storytelling as reflective of traditional society. But, much as I learned through my own grandmother, we probably need to be more conscientious about teasing away tradition as a set of obligatory customs—that is, the belief that because these are the ways things "have always been done," we ought to continue doing them—from tradition as reflective of an oral way of knowing. In other words, a tradition may be maintained because, through its inter-generational transmission, communal relations are fortified and knowledge is preserved. Individuals oriented toward high literacy may be more prone to narratively venerating subjectivity and the individualized self, with the "I" mode of being deemed superior above all others. In an altogether oral ecology, however, the focus must rest—at least if a tribe or clan wants collectively to survive through time—with a more "we" approach to being.

The epistemically oral privileging of a we-orientation breeds another intriguing question when it comes to a film like *Titanic*: Does the popularity of such a film in contemporary industrialized societies speak to our profound desire, beneath the veneer of our "I"-orientation, to reconnect with what we have lost vis-a-vis the oral group? *Titanic* and likeminded films allow us to participate in a shared recollection and public reenactment of past events. Again, that *Titanic* was also wildly popular in Afghanistan—a country second only to South Sudan in its level of nonliteracy—may say something about its more universal intelligibility as a narrative, precisely because of its operating in line with oral inflection. And since oral inflection hinges on a reticular structure, as I only just mentioned, that means *Titanic* ought to reflect other thought-related attributes characterizable as oral. Indeed it does, but you'll have to wait a little longer before we get to those. First, we need to take a detour of a somewhat different sort ....

Notes

1 Gokulsing and Dissanayake, *Indian Popular Cinema*, 29.
2 Havelock, *Preface to Plato*, 172.
3 Sobchack, "Bathos and Bathysphere," 191.
4 Abram, *Spell of the Sensuous*, 186.

References

Abram, David. *The Spell of the Sensuous: Perception and Language in a More-Than-Human World*. New York: Vintage Books, 1997.

Gokulsing, Moti K., and Wimal Dissanayake. *Indian Popular Cinema: A Narrative of Cultural Change*. Hyderabad: Orient Longman, 1998.

Havelock, Eric. *Preface to Plato*. Cambridge, MA: Belknap Press of Harvard University Press, 1963.

Sobchack, Vivian. "Bathos and Bathysphere: On Submersion, Longing, and History in *Titanic*." *Titanic: Anatomy of a Blockbuster*. Eds. Kevin S. Sandler and Gaylyn Studlar. New Brunswick, NJ: Rutgers University Press, 1999. 189–204.

15 Lists, lists, and more lists

Remember my comment earlier about how ancient oral narratives had to communicate all of their people's history, philosophy, astronomy, theology, genealogies, and gods—everything that a Viking clan or the Aranda tribe (the aboriginal inhabitants of central Australia) deemed important enough to transmit to the future generations? Well, sometimes this meant that the oral poet might resort to consolidating information and communicating it in the form of *lists*. Yes, today we may yawn and gripe at what strikes us as long, dreary, and meaninglessly dry sets of data— a litany of names, for instance, delineating how one so-and-so begot another so-and-so, who then begot so-and-so—and so on. But how else to hold onto and safeguard one's tribal roots, when one cannot rely on birth certificates, censuses, diaries, newspapers, telephone books, history books, let alone ancestry.com?

If some epics like the *Iliad* feel crammed with characters in a manner practically list-like, that may be because those characters had to be amassed and consolidated, regardless of any imprecision in the overlap of their actual time fighting in or around (or maybe *not* even in or around) the Trojan War. After all, their existence existed only by way of inclusion in the narrative. Without mention, they vanished—quite literally—from this world. No wonder, then, that Fame was such an overridingly important virtue in earlier times, including explicitly for Achilles. (The Latin word *fama* originally meant talk, rumor, or reputation, from the PIE root *bha-*, "to speak, tell, or say.") It wasn't that Fame was good for your ego. Rather, she ensured your survival in the oral–poetic realm, which is really and ultimately what made you immortal. The alternative was like what will greet the majority of us today: obscurity—although without the benefit of any continued survival through print publications, uploaded YouTube videos, or Instagram posts.

You're probably aching for an example of a list. So, here's one from the *Iliad*. It's when Homer hits the proverbial pause button on the war with the Trojans to list every Achaean (Greek) ship captain present, as well as the port from which that captain and his fleet originated:

> First came the Boeotian units led by Leitus and Peneleos:
> Arcesilaus, Prothoënor and Clonius shared command
> of the armed men who lived in Hyria, rocky Aulis,
> Schoenus, Scolus and Eteonus spurred with hills,
> Thespeia, Graea, the dancing rings of Mycalessus,
> men who lived round Harma, Ilesion and Erythrae
> and those who settled Eleon, Hyle and Peteon,
> Ocalea, Medeon's fortress walled and strong …[1]

So, did you actually read the entire list—or did you stop after about, oh, five names, before disinterestedly scanning the rest and then moving on to what I'm saying here? It's understandable, really, if you sped-read. After all, what possibly do these names mean to most of us today? But bear in mind that, when the *Iliad* was a story connected to its people orally (as distinct from its disconnected transportation through inscription into the hands of people like you and me), this was one of the only means by which one's ancestors survived through time. No wonder that we can thereby find something similar in the *Mahabharata*—that is, the poet pausing in his recounting of the "narrative proper" to offer up an extensive lineage of royalty.

Perhaps the closest way for you personally to contemporarily experience the frisson that might have been inherent in these lists would be to inventory whatever group of people comprise your particular interests or obsessions, whether these be Hollywood stars, or musicians, or Fortnight skins, or a panoply of poets and artists, or philosophers, or bodhisattvas, or sportspeople, or those on *Time*'s "100 most influential people" list .... Doing so at least drives home that, while you might only be listing their names, you carry within your brain a rich storehouse of knowledge about multiple personae, such that mention of their names alone can summon all sorts of patriotic, spiritual, historic, nationalistic, elated, or proprietary feelings.

Also bear in mind that it's these sorts of non-plot-related chunks of Homeric epic that often get excised from those bulky college-level anthologies of literature. While publishers understandably want to entice you with the richest, most dramatic, most philosophically, thematically, and ideologically pertinent portions of the *Iliad*, what they also do is disengage or unfasten the narrative from some of its more recognizably oral attributes. Purged, ironically, are the very elements or norms that define and verify the poem's initial existence as a story told by a bard like Homer. So, in spite of your possibly having pored over pages of the *Iliad* in just about any publisher's *Anthology of World Literature*, you may find some of the characteristics that we have hitherto addressed, and will continue to address, unfamiliar. If so, that's not completely surprising. In their attempt to consolidate several millennia of literature into a single volume, what better for editors to eliminate than those peculiarities of storytelling that might impede your engagement—tedious peculiarities like naming one's ancestors or digressing in ways that feel intrusive and inexplicable? After all, those publishers do so in anticipation that you, as a reading collective, will help them, as corporate entity, survive through time!

So, how present and persistent really were these lists in oral narrative? Well, enough so that, in the earliest decades of print in Western Europe—no doubt precisely because Western Europe was now becoming a print culture—Francois Rabelais would provide in his sprawling *Gargantua and Pantagruel* a satirical lineage for his hairy giant Pantagruel. That future king of the Dipsodes (people who were thirsty—for knowledge, essentially) descends from a long ancestral line, which Rabelais comically presents in an echo of Scripture:

> The first … was Chalbroth,
> Who begat Sarabroth,
> Who begat Faribroth …

This continues for an entire page-plus, before finally we reach he

> Who begat Garnet-cock,
> Who begat Grandgousier,
> Who begat Gargantua,
> Who begat the noble Pantagruel, my master.[2]

If you want to read works of fiction that animatedly and often risibly portray the clash and mingling of the oral and chirographic (i.e., handwriting) cultures with the newly emergent culture of print, you'll find no better works than those of the early modern period. Rabelais, for instance, was writing only two generations after Johannes Gutenberg's invention of movable type—and, so, we should probably not be surprised that listing is one of the conventions of narrative that he plays with endlessly. If you find Rabelais' *Gargantua and Pantagruel* heavy going, however, because of its sardonically intense grounding in medieval scholastic (university) culture, give Miguel de Cervantes' *Don Quixote* a try. Indeed, anyone who wants to get a firm handle on how print was impacting the older communication technologies of the period and sending people into an existential tizzy is probably best served by engaging with Renaissance *satire*. That literary genre often made a habit of foregrounding the narrative conventions of its age—precisely because it was flouting or mocking them.

Notes

1 Homer, *Iliad*, 115–116. The lines are 584–591 of "Book" 2.
2 Rabelais, *Gargantua and Pantagruel*, 18–20.

References

Homer. *The Iliad*. Trans. Robert Fagles. New York: Penguin Classics, 1998.
Rabelais, François. *Gargantua and Pantagruel*. Trans. M.A. Screech. New York: Penguin Books, 2006.

16 In defense of clichés and the formulaic (yes, really!)

For Theodor Adorno and Max Horkheimer, two of the leading members of the Frankfurt School of critical thought, the "culture industry" of the mid-twentieth century was a dangerous beast.[1] This was the industry that manufactured visual media, music, magazines, and other popular cultural forms, all for the express purposes of their being consumed en masse by a passively receptive consumer base. We, the willing victims, were being made to watch screens—thoughtlessly—and to listen to babbling music—childishly. These easy pleasures provided us, this entertainment as a kind of processed food, transformed us into docile beings. After all, we could escape into them so painlessly—with the industrialists all the while reaping robust profits for their manipulations. (These theorists had just survived Germany's ugly history of Nazism and, so, were understandably keen to figure out how people could remain so unresponsive in the face of atrocity.) One of the major adversaries in Adorno and Horkheimer's estimation was popular cinema, which they derided for peddling formulae and recycled elements, and for relying on what they conceived as intellectually slothful schematization.

But it takes someone with a special sensitivity to orally inflected ways of knowing—in this case, Italian historian Carlo Ginzburg—to ask if there ever really was such a thing as an entirely passive human receptor. In his micro-history of the life of a sixteenth-century miller named Mennochio, Ginzburg argues that Mennochio's obstinacy in the face of those higher-ups who accused him of heresy was evidence of his *not* being the merely passive beneficiary of someone else's ideas. True, Mennochio could read, but Ginzburg does not shirk from recognizing that Mennochio's milieu and his way of ingesting and interpreting knowledge were still fundamentally oral. Even more, Ginzburg emphatically comments on the pamphlet literature of Mennochio's century, a print form that, in tandem with the sale of almanacs, ballads, and lives of the saints, constituted the bulk of Western Europe's book trade. Pamphlet literature might appear to today's avid reader as "static, inert, and unchanging," says Ginzburg, fashioned as it was out of formulae, repetition, and continuous recycling; but we need to take into account the extent to which the predominantly oral culture of the time might have interjected *itself* into that pamphlet literature through how they used it—possibly "modifying it, reworking it, perhaps to the point of changing its very essence …"[2]

His plea that we neither dismiss this class of readers, nor assume its complete impassiveness is a good one, especially given that these attributes (the privileging of formulae, repetition, and recycling) are essential to narrative that is highly orally inflected—and for reasons that are entirely practical, economical, and existentially vital, to boot. Indeed, this may why the literati today reflexively decry these norms. But let's not be too hard on the latter. After all, would *you* deign to use any of the following pat or formulaic expressions in your writing, especially after years of having been told—nay, pretty much commanded—not to for fear of sounding dull, common, lazy, or unsophisticated?

> It was the calm before the storm.
> They lived happily ever after.
> I'm happy as a kid in a candy shop.
> I'm fit as a fiddle.
> In this day and age, we should think outside the box.
> He sailed the wine-dark sea.

Wait—what? *Wine-dark sea*? That's no pat expression! That's no cliché or platitude! And it's certainly not a formulaic expression akin to the tired "dead as a doornail" or "old as the hills." In fact, isn't that a beautiful descriptor from Homer? Doesn't he sometimes evocatively refer to the Mediterranean as the "wine-dark sea"—and so, what possibly could be cliché about that? Well, nothing, if you're living in the twenty-first century. But its frequent repetition in the *Odyssey*—much in the same way that Homer often tags that epic's protagonist "wily Odysseus"—speaks to Homer's reliance on pat phrases to fill out or appropriately round out the meter of his poem.

Milman Parry, whom I cited earlier, was instrumental in discerning Homer's repeated use of epithets, including not only the abovementioned "wine-dark sea," but other stock phrases like "there spoke clever Odysseus" and "when Dawn spread out her fingertips of rose."[3] If we want to acknowledge a Homeric aesthetics, we need admit to its being something of a mechanical or technical aesthetics. Consider, after all, that of the 27,000 hexameters, or six-foot metrical lines of verse, that comprise the *Odyssey* and the *Iliad*, repeated phrases of two words or more appear *29,000 times*[4] (that's more than one pat expression per hexameter). In fact, 90 percent of the first 15 lines of the *Iliad* (see pages 52–53) proved demonstrably formulaic—which is to say, scholars were able to match word clusters in them with others found elsewhere—*identically*—in Homer's corpus. This is how Parry's student, Albert Lord, was able to distinguish genuine oral composition by Slavic bards from any recitation of a written text. The former composition was formulaic; the latter was not.

Even more, Homer could prove somewhat indiscriminate in choosing between formulae that were otherwise metrically identical. Such is the case in his referring recurrently at one point to the *ox-eyed lady Hera* in lieu of to *Hera of the white arms*, as if, "having thought of the [former] one, he used it over again several times before it slipped from his brain."[5] In other words, he was *not* reciting memorized lines, but pulling and piecing together the narrative from his vast mental storehouse. Of course, this means that, each time he told one of his Achaean-Trojan stories, it was always slightly different. So, despite that today we preserve Homer's epics as if they were exclusive, fixed texts, no singular version of his lofty songs ever existed. A bard's emphasis was on the successful and repeated juggling of *topoi*, or traditional themes, for informing and entertaining an audience, not on producing a refined and aesthetically pleasing finished product. In this sense, an oral poem is never finished; it is always in process—that is, until someone shows up to preserve it transcriptively (in artificially frozen fashion).

Even *Beowulf*, which shows signs of not having been a direct recording of an oral performance, contains evidence of its once having been orally composed. Yes, scribal monks tinkered with the one surviving manuscript we possess of that work, even adding their own phrases—which we can tell in part through variations in spellings and linguistic forms. Nevertheless, *Beowulf* relies on diction that is not only compositionally formulaic, but on *topoi* that are found in other Old English poems, as well as in other Germanic languages. And while the ancient Hindu epic about the god Rama, the *Ramayana*, has been reworked on the page for many a century and by many a nation—India, Sri Lanka, Burma, Indonesia, China, Japan—about one-third of its *slokas* (Sanskrit couplets) show signs of formulaic expressions and traditional phraseology, paying unintended tribute thus to its origins in oral form. So, if today certain segments of society disdain stock phrases—in novels, in movies, and, perhaps most especially, in the writing of history—what they are conceding to is their own acquired inclination, whether conscious or not, to disassociate themselves from fundamentally oral composition.

These formulae were hardly customary merely because they benefitted the oral poet who was stitching together his story. Platitudes, clichés, pat phrases, commonplaces: While these may strike us today as flat, stale, and empty, they are also the most efficient means by which to transmit knowledge compactly, safely, and intelligibly—and not only from person to person, but down the longer generational line. After all, if someone were to say to you "Every dog has its—," with knee-jerk swiftness, you'd probably fill in "day." Break a—? You'd answer, "leg," of course. Don't cry over—? "Spilt milk." Better late than—? Knock on—? The cat's out of—? That's how cognitively unwasteful such sayings are.

Which is probably why we ought to provide them a less derogatory label, something like "formulaic modes of expression" or, more complimentarily, "formulary expressions."

Of course, having to rely on formulary expressions tends to perpetuate oral modes of thought—meaning that how you *have* to think unavoidably impacts how you *tend* to think. So, what, then, of those novels whose historical abandonment of the formulaic are said to have facilitated a greater intimacy with "the real"? Think Gustave Flaubert's *Madame Bovary*, for instance, or pretty much any novel assigned to you in an upper-level literature seminar. Well, we could counter that they—*we*, really—have been blinded by our own alphabetically literate belief that there is some wholly determinable, singular, objective reality to begin with. Vladimir Nabokov, for one, proclaimed that a good reader is not only someone with imagination, memory, and some artistic sense—but also a dictionary. In this way, he was conceding to the unconditional luxury of words in print. Book culture is what permits us to enrich, enliven, and downright fatten our lexicon in ways impossible in an oral context. Just imagine having internally to store 20 volumes of 171,476 words, which is what the *Oxford English Dictionary* currently contains. Still, our ability to access a source like the *OED*, especially now given the ease by which we can do so online, allows us a magnitude of vocabulary unimaginable in a non-writing ecology. So, you have to wonder: What would *Lolita* or *Pale Fire* have been had Nabokov been born somewhere near the caves of Lascaux, France, 10,000 years ago? What if Flaubert had grown up a sixteenth-century neighbor of Mennochio's? How real, then, is the realist novel—and real for whom? What questions like these bring to the fore is how our impulse for analyzing an oral epic as though its narration were the consequence of an *intrusion* of fertility myths and folktales on history or psychology is entirely wrong-headed.

Needless to say, perhaps, is that aphorisms, pat phrasings, and other such pre known nuggets of wisdom abound in 1970s–1990s Bollywood films—and nowhere more so than in their musical numbers. (Indeed, music as a genre appears more universally accepting of our oral proclivities for commonplaces

commonplaces and clichés.) Even more, when these Hindi films dramatically careen toward their climax and resolution, their dialogue almost always grows increasingly proverbial, as if conjuring through that shared language the force of tradition or of the gods. Proverbs, are the oft-familiar carriers of narrative wisdom, after all. (In the English-language context, think of sayings like "Honesty is the best policy" or "Turn the other cheek.") In fact, even language that carries the taste or bite of the didactically proverbial can work in these circumstances. True, they may strike some ears as digestibly shallow musings, but their shallowness and digestibility are altogether appropriate and even necessary in the oral context. There, words are ephemeral: Say the word "ephemeral" and before you get to the –al, the "ephemera" is gone. So, words can hardly be mulled over, let alone relished the way a Shakespearean sonnet might be from a fixed point on a page. Or, if we prefer the words of another associate of the Frankfurt School, Walter Benjamin: "A proverb, one might say, is a ruin which stands on the site of an old story and in which a moral twines about a happening like ivy around a wall."[6] So, let me provide you a few such ruins-cum-proverbial sayings pulled from the final sequence of the Hindi film *Baazigar* (a sequence, by the way, that is about to lead to a flashback): "You have only seen the crown on his head. ... Look under the thief's sleeve and you will find blood"; and, later, "You've only been pricked with a thorn. I have been wounded with a complete trident."

Lazy screenwriting? Cheap and easy melodrama achieved through words? Perhaps. But if a spectatorship prefers the use of well-worn phrases that are altogether familiar or that harken back, as this one does, to religious themes and repeated motifs, perhaps it's because these dialogues are not solely the byproduct of screenwriters bequeathing slapdash or substandard attention to their art. Why, for instance, do we adapt and embrace these sorts of sayings so completely as children, such that they come instantly to our minds decades later, in spite of our now-scornful attitude to them? If my rhetorical pleas do not strike you as sufficiently persuasive, consider the tremendous amount of energy that in the oral ecology must be invested in maintaining the learning that has come

Figure 16.1 Promotional still of Bollywood film star Madhuri Dixit in a musical number (courtesy of Alamy). Formulary epithets proliferated in the 1970s-1990s realm of the Hindi film song. *Dil deewana* (love-crazed heart) and *sapnon ki rani* (queen of my dreams) are just two of the "acoustic jingles"—as Eric Havelock refers to them in the Homeric context—whose lineage extends back 50 years. Rote knowledge of these jingles and of the songs, which were often memorized, as were long passages of dialogue, doubtlessly amplified one's connection to the material—and, so too, to the "communal soul," to the sense of oneself as part of a subjectivity larger than the mere individual. That these musical numbers typically involved the dynamic coordination of dozens of dancers similarly aided in valorizing the group and one's connection to it. Indeed, nowhere in the masala film is the acoustical-communal nature of existence perhaps more fully realized (and fetishized) than here. (If you're interested in screening a musical number from one of the biggest Bollywood blockbusters of all time, *Sholay* (Flames, dir. Ramesh Sippy, 1975), look up "Holi Ke Din" on YouTube. Or, if you're interested in seeing the above movie star in action, simply search "Madhuri Dixit dance"!)

down through the ages. Only by a community repeating over and over—and over—again what it has learned will that learning survive. In fact, I'd propose that it's not only because they're young but for similar reason that toddlers want to hear the stories they know over and over—and over—again.

If in an oral environment you want stories to live by, you kind of have to impede or deter experimentation in thought and instead pragmatically repeat—and, so, mentally etch and save— the past that is coming down to you. Again, this doesn't mean things don't change as you go; adjustments need continually to be made to accommodate present-day values, relationships, or realities. But you would hardly submit to throwing out the past. Better is to shuffle its contents in order to accommodate the new. Or, in the words of Sanskrit scholar Alf Hiltebeitel, any event or tension generated by the political or social present is "creatively grafted onto the core of oral epic's older themes and formulae."[7] Our contemporary obsession with originality, in other words—which arguably began with the eighteenth-century rise of the novel—is fundamentally the consequence of our ability to *depart* from having to carry the world, including our ancestors, in our heads. No longer do those of us in a writing environment need to conserve our (hi)story primarily by way of acoustics and memory. But in a prehistorical environment—which is to say, a prewriting one—listeners can hardly pause during the communication of a story to analyze or ruminate over its constituent parts. They can only be carried away by its sweep.

Notes

1 Max and Adorno, *Dialectic of Enlightenment.*
2 Ginzburg, *Cheese and the Worms*, xxii.
3 Abram, *Spell of the Sensuous*, 105.
4 Ibid.
5 Beye, *Ancient Epic*, 82.
6 Benjamin, "Storyteller," 93.
7 Hiltebeitel, *Rethinking India's Oral*, 26.

References

Abram, David. *The Spell of the Sensuous: Perception and Language in a More-Than-Human World.* New York: Vintage Books, 1997.

Benjamin, Walter. "The Storyteller." *Theory of the Novel: A Historical Approach.* Ed. Michael McKeown. Baltimore: Johns Hopkins University Press, 2000. 77–93.

Beye, Charles Rowan. *Ancient Epic Poetry: Homer, Apollonius, Virgil, with a Chapter on the Gilgamesh Poems.* Wauconda, IL: Bolchazy-Carducci Publishers, Inc., 2006.

Ginzburg, Carlo. *The Cheese and the Worms: The Cosmos of a Sixteenth-Century Miller.* Trans. John and Anne Tedeschi. Baltimore: Johns Hopkins University Press, 1980.

Hiltebeitel, Alf. *Rethinking India's Oral and Classical Epics: Draupadi among Rajputs, Muslims and Dalits.* Chicago: University of Chicago Press, 1999.

Horkheimer, Max, and Theodor W. Adorno, *Dialectic of Enlightenment: Philosophical Fragments.* Trans. Edmund Jephcott. Stanford, CA: Stanford University Press, 2002.

17 Repeat, recycle—and repeat (and recycle)

So, back to our classroom setting and the students who just heard Lucy recount the story of Little Red Riding Hood. Here's an easy question for them—and you: How can we make sure that the story we are telling—*our* story (meaning our history, our ancestors, our existential legacy, our moral patterns, our social taboos, indeed our very *language*)—does not get overridden by noise? Communication theory appropriately highlights that, in any act of communication, the space between the initiator of a message and its interpreter is always endangered by outside noise. This may be static, as in the case of radio or television transmission; it may be people chatting around you as you attempt to read *Pale Fire* or screen *Baazigar*, or it may even be lapses in the attention of your listener who, while you may be vigorously and vituperatively reciting Sylvia Plath's poem "Daddy," is contemplating her own life or the imminence of her lunch.

One method of ensuring that your message gets across is perhaps obvious—apparent—easy to see—and evident in full: Repetition and redundancy combat noise. Thus the prevalence in both fairy tales and lofty oral epics of repeated words, repeated phrases, and even thematic patterns repeated verbatim. Things are said once, and then several times over, either identically or in slightly different and variegated ways. As any child who has had to learn their multiplication tables by rote knows, repetition aids memory. In the case of lengthy narrative, repetition may also alert you to what's most essential of the story's content, operating thus as a kind of red flag, as a vocal annotation in the proverbial margins. "This is important because you have heard it before," it may be alerting you, or "Listen carefully, because I'm emphasizing the logical progression of this part through reiteration." Consider how many times Goldilocks repeats the phrase, "This _____ is too _____," during her trespass into the house of the three bears—as in, "This [chair/bowl/bed] is [too big/too small/just right]." And when in *Gilgamesh*, the hunter speaks of Enkidu to two different people on two separate occasions, his words are virtually identical:

> Father, a certain fellow has come from the mountains.
> He is the mightiest in the land,
> his strength is as mighty as the meteorite (?) of Anu!
> He continually goes over the mountains,
> he continually jostles at the watering place with the
>   animals,
> he continually plants his feet opposite the watering place.[1]

So, if we didn't catch the gist the first time, we likely would the second—namely, that Enkidu's totemic feature is his strength. Later in the epic, during Gilgamesh's physical descent into the Underworld, repetition and redundancy conjure an atmosphere that is not only foreboding but entirely sublime. We are made to *feel* that we are entering an alternative dimension. For the sake of brevity, let's enter that descent *in medias res*:

> Five leagues [Gilgamesh] traveled …
> dense was the darkness, light there was none,
> neither what lies ahead nor behind does it allow him to see.
> Six leagues he traveled …
> dense was the darkness, light there was none,
> neither what lies ahead nor behind does it allow him to see.
> Seven leagues he traveled …
> dense was the darkness, light there was none,
> neither what lies ahead nor behind does it allow him to see.
> Eight leagues he traveled and cried out …[2]

After a digressively philosophical wrestling with the nasty shortness of life—"For how long do we seal a document! For how long do brothers share the inheritance?"—we are brought to the final stages of Gilgamesh's otherworldly expedition:

> Eleven leagues he traveled and came out before the sun.
> Twelve leagues he traveled and it grew brilliant.
> … it bears lapis lazuli as foliage,
> bearing fruit, a delight to look upon.

Here, the repetition manages vocally to generate a terrifyingly dark tunnel through which we must ritually pass before reaching the light. Clearly, these are rhetorical tools that the oral poet can deploy for a variety of purposes.

Just as vital, to reprise, is the obligation and appeal in hearing the same story repeated over and over. Today you might think of this as something exclusive to children—in fact, research in the field of reading might speciously persuade you of such. But much as David Abram advocates based on his intimate experience with indigenous American cultures, only through ancestral stories being recounted time and again is their preservation afforded. Moreover, "this regular, often periodic repetition serves to bind the human community to the ceaseless round dance of the cosmos."[3] In other words, there's something about participating as a group through previously known stories (or dances, or songs) that renders time circular: What is known of the past is brought into the present, with the present thereby reflecting and honoring that past. No wonder that this experience can often phenomenologically converge on the magical and even sacred. These are your ancestors, after all.

By virtue of this preknowledge, oral participants don't engage in a story the way many of us today do—as, say, with mystery or detective novels, where we read in anticipation of learning what has intentionally been denied us; or because of our expectation of some "big reveal." Nor do (or, really, can) oral poets withhold information in quite the same way that writers like Dan Brown or Agatha Christie, can. While his periodic reveal of key information may be one of the reasons that we keep turning the pages, in the oral community our ears are attuned for a different reason. We come for the sake of *re*-experience, or for the experience rendered in innovatively reshuffled or variously articulated ways. Of course, an oral narrative can often multiply and metamorphose into profoundly different takes on that "original" story, depending on where one finds those derivations, both geographically as well as through time. The ancient Mongolian epic of the hunter Huuheldei Mergen Khan, for instance, exists in a number of versions that not only vary in their interpretive strategies, but range in form from 25 to 60 songs.

Is it any wonder, then, that my grandmother fussed and harrumphed when my sister, Kamala, interrupted one of her stories of Krishna in order to ask, "When did this happen?" My sister was, in effect, becoming the *noise* in my grandmother's chronicling of that beloved god's cavorting with the cowherdesses. She didn't read Kamala's attempt to analyze the story—to complicate it through questions—as sign of her more sophisticated approach to the legend; rather, Kamala was becoming a disturbance in my grandmother's attempt to communicate the tale. After all, the presumed intention in my grandmother recounting the story was so that my sister would later retell it to her own children and grandchildren. To be sure—and much as Abram notes of stories told and retold in one's childhood—my sister's future would be "inflected by the patterns of [her] own experience and the rhythms of [her] own voice"[4]; but that would be less to give her oral performance the impress of originality than actively to preserve the coherence of the culture she and her antecedents shared.

There is nothing inherently private, let alone privatized, about storytelling in a primarily oral culture. In that environment, a story is literally "of the people"—which is not to say that it's of *all* the people, mind you. Typically, the narrative belongs to a very specific community: a village, a clan, or a caste group; a tribe allied by territory, ethnicity, linguistics, or a potentate. Ownership comes not by way of copyright but by participation in the narrative's performance. (G.H. Gerould suggests that even ballads, which appeared in print clear into the nineteenth century, shared much with the fairy tale and legend, given that they, too, were taken as "common property."[5]) Indeed, our seemingly benign attribution of the *Iliad* and *Odyssey* to Homer as "author" skews the reality of oral poetry's provenance. Homer, once again, was not the author (let alone, etymologically speaking, the creator or father) of those lengthy songs, at least not any more (or less) than the bards who had been singing the same stories one year, or 20 years, or eight generations before he. (Paradoxically, ancient sculptures of Homer—which you can see by googling "classical bust of Homer"—display him with his mouth closed and his ears fully concealed beneath his hair, notwithstanding that these were the organs integral to his storytelling genius.)

Doubtlessly, there's something comforting in our being able today to attach a name to those ancient Greek poems. Being able to credit them to Homer certifies, even if only in the deepest reaches of our subconscious, our own capacity to live on far after we are gone. "Anonymous," by contrast—author of *Epic of Gilgamesh*, not to mention most Icelandic sagas, the Old French *Song of Roland*, and those fairy tales we willingly assign to the Brothers Grimm—just doesn't quite equip us with the same existential security. We prefer even the imaginarily fashioned face—like Homer's, precisely—to the historically truthful and bona fide lack of one. When someone asks you who the poet responsible for the medieval *Sir Gawain and the Green Knight* was and you have no recourse but to answer, "I don't know. Nobody does," it's not exactly a reply that reassures us about our own identity's survival through time.

What all this necessary repetition and recycling of knowledge also means is that, in the oral milieu, there can be no such thing as that evil, insidious, education-endangering act of abducting somebody else's words. Today, we of course refer to this as *plagiarism* (a word that derives from the Latin *plagium*, meaning a kidnapping!). But no such concept can exist—is even conceivable, dare I say—in a world where you want and anticipate your words being carried on others' tongues. Certainly it's no accident that the word came into popular use in English only during the

Figure 17.1 Photograph of a "one-eyed Albanian singer," from the album of Albert B. Lord, with Lord's original typewritten caption (courtesy of the Milman Parry Collection/Harvard College). The 1930s and 1950s fieldwork undertaken by Milman Parry and Lord with South Slavic heroic singers was fundamental to Parry's recognition that Homer's songs shared many of the oral underpinnings of these modern traditional poets' songs. The caption of this particular photograph sheds some fascinating and necessary, if also unintended comical, light on how oral-traditional poetry does not preclude variances in the quality of a composition, register, style, or delivery. "Sulejman Makitch is a picturesque individual," Lord notes, "but his poems were not of outstanding merit, and his knowledge of geography sadly small. One of his songs began with the line: 'In Paris, in fair Vienna ...' He kindly explained that Paris was a section of Vienna." While Makitch's description of Paris as existing in "fair Vienna" may amuse those of us who are "map literate," what difference would it have made, really, to his regional audience (unless, of course, one of his listeners was familiar with that far-off place)? Might we speculate, in fact, that some of Homer's epithetic references to geography may have been just as "empty" (or flexibly fillable, if you will) as Paris was for this Albanian singer?

sixteenth century—*after* the existence of the printing press. True, its origins lie with the ancient Roman poet Martial (d. ca. 104 CE) who, upon discovering that his work was being copied and recited by competing poets, had this to say:

> Fame has it that you, Fidentinus, recite my books to the
> crowd as if none other than your own. If you're willing that
> they be called mine, I'll send you the poems for free. If you
> want them to be called yours, buy this one, so that they won't
> be mine.[6]

In other words, if Martial equated Fidentinus' deviant act with
that of "stealing his slaves" (which he did), his animosity was
foremost stirred by his having been denied his proper payment.
Writing had turned words into a physical commodity, with all
that latter term's implications of ownership, proprietary rights,
and a thing that was yours to trade independent of any group.
In a world where words were entirely ephemeral, on the other
hand—gone at the very moment of their utterance—who could
possibly materially snatch them, in order to put a fence around
them and call them one's own?

Notes

1 *Epic of Gilgamesh*. Both passages occur in Tablet 1.
2 Ibid. These lines are from Table IX, as are the lines that follow shortly.
3 Abram, *Spell of the Sensuous*, 186.
4 Ibid., 181.
5 Quoted in Chambers, *English Literature*, 179.
6 Quoted in Anderson, "Martial 1.29," 119.

References

Abram, David. *The Spell of the Sensuous: Perception and Language in a
    More-Than-Human World*. New York: Vintage Books, 1997.
Anderson, Peter. "Martial 1.29: Appearance and Authorship." *Rheinisches
    Museum für Philologie*, Neue Folge, 149. Bd., H. 1 (2006): 119–122.
Chambers, E.K. *English Literature at the Close of the Middle Ages*. New York:
    Oxford University Press, 1945.
The Epic of Gilgamesh. Trans. Maureen Gallery Kovacs. Electronic
    edition by Wolfe Carnahan. Academy for Ancient Texts. Retrieved
    August 8, 2017, from www.ancienttexts.org/library/mesopotamian/
    gilgamesh/tab1.htm.

18 Whence the "traditional"?

There's something else that arguably combats the noise in a story's oral transmission through time: those *topoi* long handed down and which we often call "traditional"—precisely because they appear across so much lengthy oral poetry of yore. They're there no matter whether we are in Gilgamesh's Mesopotamia, or Sita's ancient India, or Achilles' ancient Greece. (Nathaniel Hawthorne commented that traditions were impossible for any one individual to invent, as ultimately it took a century to make them.) These traditional themes—such as the search for wisdom—are also often associated with a given motif, such as a hero's descent into the underworld. To be sure, their durability resides in part in their attunement to existential questions that obsess us today no less than they did the ancients: Why are we here? Why must we die? Where do we go after? What makes a good ruler? How do we explain the bad things that happen to us—our struggles with the land, with starvation, with war, with all manner of external aggressors?

The Swiss psychiatrist Carl Jung, whom we met briefly when discussing *Star Wars*, called these *archetypes* (from *arche*, as in the "first or original," and *typos*, "form"); and he did so because of these types' cross-cultural omnipresence, which to him suggested that they were deeply embedded in our collective unconscious. Such archetypes include, though are hardly limited to, the hero, the hero's negative shadow, and the wise old man who can often foresee what is to come; the idealized mother figure; the quest;

death and rebirth; the wanderer who finds his way, the magician who changes the world, and the orphan who survives. Joseph Campbell, the comparative mythologist whom we discussed in light of his influence on the script of *Star Wars*, later demonstrated how the myths that had endured through time, both in the east and west, shared a structure that hinged on an archetypal hero's journey. This hero's passage characteristically progressed from a call to adventure, to his engagement with helpers and mentors, as well as with challenges and temptations, before his finally undergoing an enduring transformation that eventually led to his return home.

Lest you still think this is something that no longer applies in the modern world, check out the visual journalist Patrick Garvin's online "Your All-Purpose Guide to Epic Movies" graphic, which delightfully illustrates how uncannily Campbell's categorization of the characters central to quest myths underpins so many modern Hollywood films. "If you ever get the feeling you're seeing the same film over and over," Garvin quips, "well, history agrees with you." I can't include Garvin's graphic in this book because, while it's legal for me to quote Garvin—as well as to tell you that the films he breaks down on the basis of their archetypes are *The Matrix*, *Star Wars*, *Finding Nemo*, *Harry Potter*, and *Lord of the Rings*—the actual images from the films are the property of someone else. There's a certain irony in this, considering that notions of copyright—and the very possibility of someone actually owning images or words—would have struck the oral communities who "invented" these archetypes as altogether baffling.

Of course, putting a protagonist on the road is also the best means by which to weave all the strands of an oral narrative together. Why? Because doing so creates an entirely situational story rather than a contemporary recording of events that is dry, distanced, and willfully abstract. Or, in less dry, distanced, and willfully abstract terms: In the situational context, people *do* things, they *go* places, they encounter difficulties that they must *overcome*. Just imagine a historian today writing this way! In fact, these were the very conventions of oral epic, resilient as they were, that led many scholars for many centuries to deem the *Iliad* entirely fictitious rather than a story bearing the seeds of actual historical events. But I'll once again posit that most oral epics owe their origins to real events, though these events unavoidably come down to us bearing generations of accretions, modifications, and shrouding by time. My rationale is simple—though I would hardly call it simplistic: Would an exclusively oral clan or tribe have devoted so much time and careful attention to preserving what had, from the beginning, been entirely fictitious? Still, these stories did have to be packaged in ways that would ensure their perpetuation, which sometimes required them to take on qualities that. to our contemporary eyes, seem less "real."

Literary theorists Robert Scholes and Robert Kellogg tried to get at this phenomenon in a slightly different and, frankly, more compellingly curious fashion: They advised that readers resist the customary route of presuming that a historical account had been given an epic treatment, such that it bore "the intrusion of imaginative distortion and contamination by non-historical myths and *topoi*." Rather, they promoted starting from the proposition that the historical event itself had intruded "upon the traditional stock of myths and *topoi*" and, so, "some sort of readjustment in the tradition [was required] to accommodate it."[1] From this vantage point, any historical event considered significant enough to merit narrative incorporation has to be *fit into* the traditional stock of themes central to so many oral epics from across the world: the Assembly, the Arming of the Hero, the Hero's Return, the Test of the Wife. Either way you look at it, whether as history intruding on epic or the other way around, the traditional, story-making reserve of myths and *topoi* remains of essence—and, again, universally so, with respect to the ways that it may adjust or "distort" history. We'll get to some of the very concrete and particular ways that this happens in just a few pages—ways that will almost certainly compel you to reflect on your own notions of what makes a story "feel" like myth.

If you're willing to accept that ways of *having* to tell stories in an oral, prehistorical milieu may be as paramount as any collective unconscious, then it's worth our putting Jung into conversation, even if only imaginatively, with the social psychologist A.R. Luria. Luria traveled in the early 1930s to some of the remoter areas of the former Soviet Union, where, at the suggestion of famed psychologist Lev Vygotsky, he undertook fieldwork with unlettered and semilettered peasants. What Luria discovered is that the process of ratiocination, of reasoning—in this case, for the sake of drawing inferences—was not only unattractive to those peasants; it even appeared to them as an impractical endeavor. What they deemed cognitively important in the world was based foremost on functional relevance. They exhibited little desire to shift abstractly—and, so, meaninglessly, as far as they were concerned—from one category to another.

For instance, one subject—documented as "Abdurakhm., age 37, from remote Kashgar village, illiterate"[2]—was asked what kind of bears there were in Novaya Zemaya, which was in the Far North, he'd been told, where all bears were white. He responded that he didn't know: "I've seen a black bear. I've never seen any others." When pressed on this syllogism regarding the bears in Novaya Zemaya, he stated, "We always speak only of what we see; we don't talk about what we haven't seen." "But what do my words imply?" demanded the researcher. "Well, it's like this," Abdurakhm. replied, "our tsar isn't like yours, and yours isn't like ours. Your words can be answered only by someone who was there, and if a person wasn't there he can't say anything on the basis of your words."[3] His response may seem curious, maybe even bemusing to you; but it was hardly an anomaly. Repeatedly, subjects were averse to discussing topics that went beyond their personal experience.

But this makes sense when one recalls that, in the oral economy, utterances are tied to action; they are fundamentally bound to situations—whether journeying somewhere, or felling trees, or eating, or dreaming, or even telling stories to others over a meal. Inscription is what allows words to become ever-more independent of activity: to be mused over and inspected in ever-greater detail; to be taken out of context and also put within. Speech, as anthropologist Jack Goody would later declare, becomes in the context of writing wrested from "'occasion'; it becomes timeless. Nor is it attached to a person; on paper, it becomes more abstract, more depersonalised."[4] Or, in the words of book historian Henri-Jean Martin, "Written discourse incited the individual to adopt a cold view of the world and his fellows, a view detached from contingencies and repressing sensitivity."[5]

Cold? Depersonalized? How bleak! How offensive! Surely, you, dear reader, don't think of yourself (as I don't think of myself) as living in and experiencing the world in such an impersonal, alienated, and responsively repressed manner. In fact, most readers would contend (and have it contended about them by neurologists) that engaging with print narratives—novels, biographies, historical fiction, and the like—makes one more sensitive to one's fellow human beings, not less. Like a kind of glorious alchemy, your sense of empathy in your actual life feels heightened, not diminished, by your willing immersion into other people's stories in books. And yet, isn't there is a grand irony in our turning to a medium that physically *separates* us from others, in order to feel bound to them more strongly?

By no means am I trying to glorify or nostalgically privilege oral culture. Requisite face-to-face contact, the unavoidable necessity of having to deal directly with others through word of mouth, comes with its own set of limitations and frustrations. There's, for one, the inordinate lack of personal privacy that orality mandates, as well as the possible dearth of space for individual expression, since too much eccentric individualism might go against the stubborn status quo. Meanwhile, so cherished is this individualism in writing cultures that, in some instances, it's considered a veritable right. Clearly, any change in medium is a two-way street, a "Faustian bargain," as media ecologist Neil Postman once acknowledged.[6] That is, technological change always brings with it both advantages and disadvantages—proves harmful to some *and* beneficial to others. In no small measure, this is because some new technologies don't just add something to a culture; they have the potential to *change everything*.

Notes

1 Scholes and Kellogg, *Nature of Narrative*, 40.
2 Luria, *Cognitive Development*, 108.
3 Ibid., 109.
4 Goody, *Domestication*, 44.
5 Martin, *History and Power*, 510.
6 Postman, "Five Things We Need."

References

Goody, Jack. *The Domestication of the Savage Mind.* Cambridge: Cambridge University Press, 1977.
Luria A.R. *Cognitive Development: Its Cultural and Social Foundations.* Trans. Martin Lopez-Morillas and Lynn Solotaroff. Ed. Michael Cole. Cambridge: Harvard University Press, 1976.
Martin, Henri-Jean. *The History and Power of Writing.* Trans. Lydia G. Cochrane. Chicago: University of Chicago Press, 1994.
Postman, Neil. "Five Things We Need to Know About Technological Change." Talk delivered in Denver, CO, March 28, 1998. Retrieved April 2, 2015, from http://web.cs.ucdavis.edu/~rogaway/classes/188/materials/postman.pdf.
Scholes, Robert and Robert Kellogg. *The Nature of Narrative.* Oxford: Oxford University Press, 1968.

19 The acoustic landscape

While the last phrase of the previous chapter—"they have the potential to *change everything*"—may have struck you as histrionic, bear in mind that you don't hear many a child in industrialized nations proclaiming, "Mom, I want to be a bard." By contrast, "Mom, I want to be a writer"—that's pretty common. What's reflected in that professional shift is a comprehensive redirection in the nature of narrative. Extended narrative, quite simply, no longer has its fundamental, long-term residence in the breath. How, consequently, for its construction, focus, and even purpose *not* to change?

For tens of thousands of years, human breath was the most profound expression of human being. This isn't me talking—it's the French prehistoric art specialist Michel Lorblanchet. Even when it comes to those Paleolithic paintings at Lascaux, with their massive ochre bulls and stencils of human hands, human breath, says Lorblanchet, "literally breathe[d] life onto a cave wall. The painter projected his being onto the rock."[1] We've lost much of the significance of the breath to earlier cultures, given that, with writing, our sensory focus has migrated from the mouth and the ear—which is to say, from the acoustical world—to that of the eye. This sensory resettlement didn't happen overnight. Even as late as the Middle Ages, much as had been the case in antiquity, reading was not done principally with the eyes, but with the lips. As Benedictine monk and scholar Jean Leclercq recounts, readers pronounced what they saw out loud and, so, were listening with their ears and hearing, in effect, "the voices of the pages."[2] (There's a famous, if halfway apocryphal story of St. Augustine being shocked to find his mentor St. Ambrose reading, of all things, *silently!*) Time was necessary—much as it is for a child learning the skill—for reading to become fully detached from the muscle memory that word pronouncement stimulates, such that words could become increasingly experienced in ocular ways.

It's true, of course, that reading remains intimately, and even inextricably, bound to speech, even when we no longer move our lips in the exercise of the skill. The founder of modern linguistics, Ferdinand de Saussure, famously compared human language to a sheet of paper. If one side is thought, the reverse side is sound—with the two incapable of being disentangled from each other:

> Just as it is impossible to take a pair of scissors and cut one side of the paper without at the same time cutting the other, so it is impossible in a language to isolate sound from thought, or thought from sound.[3]

In this way, even writing continues to involve both signs and sounds. But we can—and, in what follows, we *will*—attempt, at least intellectually, to continue removing the layers of writing that have attached themselves like so many centuries of sediment to our relationship to narrative. Or, in the more forceful words of sociologist Derrick de Kerckhove, "The fact is that, as western people, we have become gradually deaf through no fault of our own, through the rewiring of our nervous system by literacy."[4] (Earlier, literary theorist Mikhail Bakhtin called this "mute perception."[5]) As for our current obsession with computer screens, smart phones, virtual reality, and the like: That seems only to affirm the proposition that we are increasingly rewiring ourselves for the visual, with the once-preeminence of the oral/aural forced into the background, like some supporting music track.

So, let's try to get back to when—for so many millennia—our experience of narrative was primarily acoustic, with the spoken word as central. Let's start with the fact that hearing comes long before seeing in the human species. The in-utero child hears and relates tactilely to its environment before ever opening its eyes (which, by the way, only occurs after those nine months in the womb). By week 24, the fetus will even begin turning its head in response to voices and noise. Surely, it's no mere accident that, in our anatomical formation, the aural supersedes the visual.

True, you could say this evolutionary process has to do with the relative darkness of the womb and, so, the lack of any need for sight while the infant is developing in utero. So, then, let's transition to our bodily existence *outside* that initial place of security. Why are we anatomically engineered so that our ears, because of their positioning at our sides, can hear noises all around us, while our eyes are physiologically situated in front of our face? If the visual is so crucial, why are we physiologically programmed so that we can only see what is directly in front of us? Should we assume that, once upon a time, we no more saw our animate surroundings—canyons, streams, mountains, wild beasts, groves of fruit trees—than we *heard* them? Is it possible their dynamism was at one time as audible for us as it was visible? According to David Abram, place for an oral culture is never merely inert, a passive setting upon which active human events occur. Rather, place, he remarks, is "*an active participant in those occurrences*" (the italics are his). In fact, "by virtue of its underlying and enveloping presence, the place may even be felt to be the source, the primary power that expresses itself through the various events that unfold there."[6]

What's fascinating about these statements is how intensely they resonate apropos those late-twentieth-century Bollywood movies I've been talking about. While suggesting that a medium as strikingly visual as film would harbor or pivot significantly on sound as experienced in the oral context, try sitting with your eyes closed through some of the most iconic blockbusters of the last century: *Mother India* (1957), *Sholay* (lit. Flames, 1975), *Qayamat Se Qayamat Tak* (lit. From Doom till Doom, 1988), *Hum Aapke Hain Koun …!* (lit. Who Am I to You?, 1994). Chances are good that you will swiftly become aware of the intensity of their acoustics. Virtually every frame of these films—and here I'm speaking quite literally—comes accompanied by some sort of audible consort, with the sound often aggrandized even, for aural effect. A colloquy between two brothers will be delivered with exaggerated moral fervor, much as a heroine will unabashedly soliloquize to her own reflection in a mirror. An image, however still, will be accompanied by the soaring and, yes, emotion-ascribing harmonies of a musical soundtrack (e.g., "now we are sad," "now we are hopeful"), with assorted clamorous sound effects frequently auguring the arrival of the human utterance. There is rarely, if ever, in these films a moment of complete and extended silence. So, yes, film is a visual medium—but that doesn't mean movies can't also sometimes submit to the epistemically oral ascendancy of the voice.

Let's take as a single, concrete example the case of verbalized oaths in these movies. They come highly dramatized—*melo*dramatized, actually—with sons pledging to avenge their mothers in stentorian tones (or, better yet, while sliding their palm down a sharp scimitar); and heroines vowing in piercing tones to sacrifice themselves for the sake of preserving their family's honor. According to Ivan Illich and Barry Sanders, authors of *ABC: The Alphabetization of the Popular Mind*, oaths are one the forms of utterances that are "most carefully guarded against change." That's because, through being audibly pledged, an oath makes the words visible—"not on paper, but in the living body of the person concerned. It incarnates the veracity of what he is saying."[7] For Illich and Sanders, this captures the very essence of an oral mentality: truth as lodged in a ritualized enactment of speech. No less interesting for us, given our earlier emphasis on the primacy and even agency of place in the oral milieu, is those writers' observation that, clear into the eighteenth century in Europe, oaths took place primarily in the open air. The reason? Because that's where you went if you wanted those words manifest before the gods, the spirits, or the dead.

In the 1970s–1990s masala film context, such oath-exhorting scenes often come aurally accessorized with a sudden blustering of wind, or of temple bells or some other natural or religiously tinged totemic force that signals the oath's existence as truth-incarnate.

In this way, the oaths acquire a kind of iconographic sacredness, a ceremonial close-to-godliness and set-apartness. In communion with the living environment, the speaking human's words are thereby validated and reinforced. In other words, this environment breathes, it speaks, it offers up agreement—or repudiation, in the case of villains. No less than the characters, it concedes and castigates, it bristles with life. Perhaps silence of any extended sort, then, is virtually impossible—because what would that signal but narrative-ecological-divine death?

Equally noteworthy is that these films' climactic showdowns—typically the consequence of those earlier-delivered oaths—transpire in settings that explicitly conjure *sacred space*. Such settings may include old, crumbling temple grounds now subsumed by jungle and howler monkeys, or the eerily empty inner main court of the historic Red Fort. A protagonist's final clash may proceed from the gallery atop a mosque's minaret, or in sight of a Vedic fire engirdled by strung marigold garlands in anticipation of a marital ceremony—or, in a nationalistic extension of these, on an army field where the Indian flag flaps and waves robustly. In these cases, too, the environment becomes a living thing, imbued with all the aura and expectation of duty, tradition, country, and, if executed properly, communal sanctification. What's also accomplished by these means is that the present gets meaningfully telescoped with the *eternal*. The past here is not experienced as a mere and historical has-been, but as an integral part of the continuing present. And since we, as individuals, are enmeshed only for the briefest time in Time, with the latter continuing quite beyond and without us, we may well *want* in the oral milieu for our stories to belong to that larger, longer, and even hallowed mythological realm.

Notes

1 Quoted in Bahn, *Cambridge Illustrated*, 126

2 Quoted in Martin, *History and Power*, 73.

3 This quote from Ferdinand de Saussure, as well as the one below, I borrow from Andrew Robinson's lively *The Story of Writing*, 17.

4 De Kerckhove, *Skin of Culture*.
5 Bakhtin, *Dialogic Imagination*, 3. The essay in particular is "Epic and the Novel."
6 Abram, *Spell of the Sensuous*, 162.
7 Illich and Sanders, *ABC*, 33–34.

References

Abram, David. *The Spell of the Sensuous: Perception and Language in a More-Than-Human World*. New York: Vintage Books, 1997.

Bahn, Paul G. *The Cambridge Illustrated History of Prehistoric Art*. Cambridge: Cambridge University Press, 1998.

Bakhtin, M.M. *The Dialogic Imagination: Four Essays*. Ed. Michael Holquist. Trans. Caryl Emerson and Michael Holquist. Austin: University of Texas Press, 1981.

De Kerckhove, Derrick. *The Skin of Culture: Investigating the New Electronic Reality*. Ed. Christopher Dewdney. London: Kogan Page, 1997.

Illich, Ivan, and Barry Sanders, *ABC: The Alphabetization of the Popular Mind*. San Francisco: North Point Press, 1988.

Martin, Henri-Jean. *The History and Power of Writing*. Trans. Lydia G. Cochrane. Chicago: University of Chicago Press, 1994.

Robinson, Andrew. *The Story of Writing: Alphabets, Hieroglyphs & Pictograms*. London: Thames & Hudson, 1995.

20 Ancestors and alienation

Okay, so perhaps this is all starting to sound a bit too religious: cyclicality, temple bells, incarnation, and all that. But think about what a *speaking* landscape must mean to an oral culture: a landscape that senses us, responds to us, sound-effectually nods us its permission (or vehemently denies us the same). For, a place that speaks to us, a place from which we seek and garner permission, is both invoking and also paying inadvertent obeisance to our *ancestors*, to all those of our group who came before us. This may be a lineage based on family bloodlines, on historical pedigree, or even on our gods or nation-state.

Today, we have such relationships soldered for us through print—in the form of histories, holy books, biographies, philosophy tracts. In the oral milieu, however, those sanctified environments arguably serve as what historian of religions Mircea Eliade called the *omphalos*, the navel, which binds and connects us to that larger, longer, and even hallowed mythological realm.[1] No less relevant—though certainly less mystical—is Eric Havelock's commentary on oral minstrelsy in the ancient Greek context. After all, those ancient bards' songs likewise address and project a "group-sense of history," one that does not seek to prophesy change so much as to "affirm continuity."[2] It's hardly accident, thus, that in the masala films I've been citing, often their final acts are immediately preceded by, or include, the presence of flashbacks (such as recollection of a wounded mother, or murdered father, or a family fortune lost)—and, so, quite literally enmesh the past with the present.

Sounding too schmaltzy now for some of you? If so, I can see why. But consider the scenario from the epistemically oral purview. What if you, in this circumstance and as a single individual, were to be *severed* from the umbilical cord that ties you to your community? Worse yet, what if ultimately you were cast out of your exclusively oral culture—exiled forever and forced to wander on your own? No less would your banishment be from your physical community than existentially from your communal past. Gone would be your participation in the rites and rituals so prevalent in the stories—and prevalent no less for the sake of keeping those rites and rituals "alive" than because they reflect the ultimate in shared experience: funerary and marital customs, the forging of political alliances, preparations for war. Gone, too, would be the echoes of your more extended being, which resonated through the recitation of your ancestors' names and the stories of their exploits as recounted by your clan's poets. And gone would be your rootedness to the particular places and ecologies that gave rise to those experienced events.

The Anglo-Saxons certainly understood the heavy anguish of this phenomenon. In the anonymous "The Wanderer," a song whose pedigree dates back to preliterate culture, its speaker acknowledges being *seledrēorig*, which literally translates as "hall-sad."[3] The hall—or mead hall, as some readers might recollect from reading *Beowulf*—was paramount to the Anglo-Saxon culture of storytelling. How much so? Well, consider that the Old English word for "narrative" or "history," *recednes*, is a compound word built out of the place where it got told—*reced*, for building, house, palace, or hall.[4] *Scop* was the term in the Anglo-Saxon tradition for the poet who recounted those narratives in the mead hall. Indeed, so integral was his role that he is alluded to several times in *Beowulf* and extolled for having sung "from time to time, in a clear / Pure voice."[5] His singing, about which we are merely told, is nevertheless interspersed with long, detailed soliloquies by other individuals who recount what *they* know about Beowulf—having heard many a tale about that hero's deeds, his strength, and his boastfulness. (Here, then, is one way that aspects of the story, including Beowulf's own presence in it, are stitched together.)

The medievalist Eric Jager enticingly refers to the expression exhibited in this oral Germanic tradition as being even more specifically *pec*toral—which is to say, chest-centered no less than mouth-centered.[6] In this epical environment, Jager argues, people believed their thoughts to reside in their "spirit-chests." Thus when Beowulf is instructed to identify himself upon his arrival on Danish soil, in preparation for offering up his familial lineage and his deeds (which he will do more than once), the words are "unlock[ed]" from "deep in his breast."[7]

Nowhere, perhaps, is the polyphonic significance of the scop to Anglo-Saxon culture made more apparent than in the passage that follows this deep unlocking. Its lines preface a digression, one of those excursions that is the byproduct of a story being embedded within the principle story. This one will narratively flash us back to the adventurous "old song" of Siegmund and the dragon. First, though, we are told of the soldier who is on the verge of recollecting that song:

> And sometimes a proud old soldier
> Who had heard songs of the ancient heroes
> And could sing them all through, story after story,
> Would weave a net of words for Beowulf's
> Victory, tying the knot of his verses
> Smoothly, swiftly, into place with a poet's
> Quick skill, singing his new song aloud
> While he shaped it, and the old songs as well—Siegmund's
> Adventures, familiar battles fought ...[8]

For certain, I could have, and perhaps ought to have, included this passage in the chapter having to do with oral epic's necessary dedication to weaving the past with the present. But look at how intriguingly the anonymous singer of "our" version of *Beowulf* inserts the present—the "new song" about Beowulf as imagined by a "proud old soldier"—into this overarching song which *is* Beowulf's, though with a pause provided now so that we might participate in that older song about Siegmund.

Figure 20.1 Benjamin Bagby performing *Beowulf* as a scop—which is to say, performing the epic "pectoral style." Courtesy of Benjamin Bagby/Photograph by Hilary Scott. While his performances can be dramatically charged in keeping with oral delivery, Bagby ultimately has to rely on a fixed text in order to accommodate his international audiences. For instance, when presenting in Moscow, the text of his Old English performance was projected behind him in Russian. Still, no performance is ever exactly the same, with his use of dynamics and rhythmic elements having evolved over the years.[9] In this way, more in keeping with a scop, he presents somewhat flexible versions of the portions of the story he recounts. This sort of flexibility would, of course, have been deeply essential in a culture where one couldn't possibly memorize a lengthy song, in no small measure because no fixed text in writing existed! Incidentally, the six-string harp Bagby uses is based on remains of a seventh-century instrument excavated from an Alemannic German nobleman's grave.

Notes

1 See, in particular, his book *Patterns in Comparative Religion*.
2 Havelock, *Preface to Plato*, 105.
3 See Richard Marsden's provided gloss of the poem.

4 From J.R.C. Hall's *Concise Anglo-Saxon Dictionary O-S*, in *Concise Anglo-Saxon Dictionary for the Use of Students.*
5 These lines, and all subsequent lines from *Beowulf*, are from the translation by Burton Raffel. The lines here appear at 496–497 (38).
6 Jager, "Speech and the Chest," 845.
7 This appears at lines 258–259 (31).
8 This passage appears at lines 867–875 of the poem (50).
9 Seth Cooper, personal communication.

References

Beowulf. Trans. Burton Raffel. New York: Signet Classic, 1999.

Eliade, Mircea. *Patterns in Comparative Religion.* Trans. Rosemary Sheed. Lincoln: University of Nebraska Press, 1996.

Hall, John R. Clark. *A Concise Anglo-Saxon Dictionary for the Use of Students.* Project Gutenberg. Release date 7 March 2010. Retrieved August 9, 2017, from www.gutenberg.org/files/31543/31543-h/files/dict_os.html.

Havelock, Eric. *Preface to Plato.* Cambridge, MA: Belknap Press of Harvard University Press, 1963.

Jager, Eric. "Speech and the Chest in Old English Poetry: Orality or Pectorality?" *Speculum* 64, 4 (October 1990): 845–859.

Marsden, Richard. *The Cambridge Old English Reader.* Cambridge: Cambridge University Press, 2004.

21 Alienation and participation

Old songs, new songs—and, yes, even future songs that will compel a restructuring of where the old songs belong: This is the living nature of storytelling in oral cultures. So, too, is the fact that with each recounting, any story—every story— is unavoidably reshaped, rewoven, and, so, never exactly the same story twice. The continuously evolving, ephemeral nature of oral narrative would certainly make any forced or accidental wanderer's exile a particularly terrible *wyrd*. That's the Old English word for "fate" or "personal destiny" (it's also a word that, with time and the influx to England of the French-speaking Normans, got downgraded to our contemporary *weird*). In effect, those in *Beowulf* who are "seated along their mead-benches"[1] are the very knots in the net that the scop of "our" *Beowulf* is composing. Participation comes necessarily in the verbal telling—and, so, where there is wordlessness, we might say, there is only absence of story. That's not to say that epic and folk narratives aren't fully capable of silence or pausal depth. But as John Miles Foley points out—he was an expert in comparative oral traditions—such pauses and breaks from sound are themselves experienced as *utterance*. That is, they serve not to provoke a listener's private thoughts, but as "institutionalized cues that help to channel audience reaction."[2]

If there's something our contemporary storytelling has lost, it's this participatory aspect, which binds the storytellers both in and of *Beowulf* to their audience. True, the feasting, laughing, and drinking that nominally occur in the same setting as the storytelling—the mead hall in *Beowulf*'s case, a banquet in the *Odyssey*'s—may suggest a certain superficiality in the extent of the listeners' participation. Sometimes, however, we are fortunate enough to find oral epics where an actual audience's vocal participation in the story has been included as part of the transcription. Such is the case of the *Epic of Sundiata*, which recounts the heroic rise of the thirteenth-century founder of the old Malian Kingdom of the Manden (with attention paid, of course, to his ancestors too). Believe it or not, this epic also comes to us narrated explicitly by a named oral storyteller-historian, the griot Mamoudou Kouyaté. (*Griot* is a French word, incidentally; the indigenous term for a professional bard would be *jeli* or *jali*.)

Kouyaté even spoke directly about his professional role as a griot when in the presence, in 1960, of his transcriber, historian Djibril Tamsir Niane. He called himself a "master in the art of eloquence," with forebears who since "time immemorial" had acted "in the service of the Keita princes of Mali."[3] How fortunate that we can actually hear firsthand from a *jeli*! And, so, in spite of Kouyaté's words bearing only a tangential relationship to this chapter's theme of participation, let us hear his take on what it means to be an oral storyteller:

> [W]e are vessels of speech, we are the repositories which harbor secrets many centuries old. … [W]ithout us the names of kings would vanish into oblivion, we are the memory of mankind; by the spoken word we bring to life the deeds and exploits of kings for younger generations.
>
> I derive my knowledge from my father Djeli Kedian, who also got it from his father; history holds no mystery for us. …
>
> I teach kings the history of their ancestors so that the lives of the ancients might serve them as an example, for the world is old, but the future springs from the past. …
>
> My word is pure and free of all untruth; it is the word of my father; it is the word of my father's father; I will give you my father's words just as I received them; royal griots do not know what lying is. When a quarrel breaks out between

tribes it is we who settle the difference, for we are the depositaries of oaths which the ancestors swore.
Listen …
Listen …

As for the politics inherent in these griots' attachment to houses of royalty (as were also the *skalds* of Scandinavia): We shall return to that sticky point in an ensuing chapter. For now, I want to focus on something D.T. Niane's transcription of this Mali epic *doesn't* include, but which a later recording in 1968 does: the recurrent and dynamic call-and-response representative of the poet's audience. This published edition and translation of the epic—which, nice to see, gives some authorial credit to its tale-teller, Fa-Digi Sisòkò—goes by the published title of *The Epic of Son-Jara*. It runs 3,084 lines, and begins at the very beginning, which is to say with the birth of humankind.[4] But what's most notable about this version, to resume with our participation theme, is that it parenthetically incorporates the vocal responses to Sisòkò's performance. And not just any responses. These ones are officially part of the performance, given that they are uttered by a *naamu*-sayer, who is oftentimes an apprentice bard. In the following excerpt, our hero Son-Jara—the original "lion king," by the way—defeats Surnamuru at a place called Kulu-Kòrò, where Surnamuru's spirit is said still to dwell:

Son-Jara held [Surnamuru] at bladepoint: (Indeed)
   "We have taken you, Colossus!"   (That's the truth)
   "We have taken you!"   (Indeed)
Surnamuru dried up on the spot, nyònyòwu!   (Indeed)
He has become the sacred fetish of Kulu-Kòrò.   (Indeed)
The Bambaraa worship that now, my father.
Susu Mountain Sumamuru,
He became the sacred fetish.   (That's the truth, indeed,
                                                              father, yes, yes, yes, yes)[5]

Call and response is identified foremost, and certainly in its most sophisticated and deeply rooted forms, with West African oral epic and song—which also accounts for its having found its way into gospel, jazz, blues, and hip-hop. Nevertheless, the practice extends to other cultures, and ones quite beyond the continent of Africa or the scattered shores of its diaspora. You can find it a part of First Nations storytelling as well as in Hindu performances, and it's also an essential component in the recital of Sufi devotional songs known as *qawwali*. Not only does call and response ensure an audience's sustained engagement with a recounted narrative; the practice also cements and certifies collective ownership of that story. (Again, we're reminded that neither copyright protection nor plagiarism can exist in the oral and, thus, decidedly nonprivatized milieu.)

Yes, audiences today may watch in anticipated, respectful silence the boisterously live—and, indeed, pectoral—performance of *Beowulf* that Benjamin Bagby offers to the strum of his medieval harp; but chances are high that, in *Beowulf*'s pre-inscription days, any performance rarely, if ever, came without vocal responses from its audience: commentary, criticism, exclamations of approval, interjections, perhaps even the occasional expletive. (Check out YouTube for a taste of the orally inflected pectorality with which Bagby performs. Not only that, if you watch long enough, you'll get a glimpse of his wide-eyed but utterly tight-lipped audience.)

Many of us who exist today in industrialized societies have lost touch with this aspect of theatrical performance, except perhaps in the sanctuary of the sports arena. Yelling at the stage; commenting out loud on a story as it progresses, whether to express one's agreement—*That's the truth! Indeed!*—or an empathetic sensation of horror or despair—*No! Don't open that door!*—have become signs of gross disrespect rather than of intense engagement. Could this be due to the long-term cultural influence of silent reading and our own sustained immersion in that practice? On the other hand, twentieth-century history of movie theaters in places like Egypt, India, and Iran testifies to locales where audiences could still interact in high and animated oral fashion. As film scholar Hamid Naficy describes of the Iranian theaters of his youth, their audiences' vigorous articulations at the screen heightened the contentiousness of the viewing experience. People would not hesitate to tell the actors on screen what they should do next: "Oh, watch out, he is behind you," "Yeah, punch him hard in the stomach, hit him, hit him."[6]

Filmmaker and film theorist Viola Shafik notes something similar of the previous century's third-class theaters in Egypt (where Hindi films were often shown). Not only did the audiences know the films largely by heart, they interacted energetically with the action, even repeating or commenting on that action during the projection.[7]

Heckling characters, shouting at the screen, commenting publicly on the narrative as it proceeds: All these are activities in keeping with orally inflected participation. Why might that be? Because sound is what is dynamic to oral cultures—or to "verbomotor" cultures, as anthropologist Marcel Jousse once termed them.[8] So, while cultures reared on alphabetic literacy might consider individuals from these cultures as "making all too much of speech," in the words of Walter J. Ong, "as overvaluing and overpracticing rhetoric,"[9] that is largely because those alphabetically literate cultures have come to rely evermore on nonverbal, visual input. We need wonder, consequently, if the discipline of film studies has downplayed the significance of aurality to films like those from Naficy's childhood, given that so much of our film-viewing now takes place in the noncommunal privacy of our own homes or offices.

Believe it or not, our engagement with the plays of William Shakespeare may have gone this increasingly, if accidentally "literized" direction. Historian Lawrence Levine's meticulously researched *Highbrow/Lowbrow* details how Shakespeare's plays were both performed and responded to in nineteenth-century America. While Levine asserts that he is most certainly not nostalgic for the "disorderly crowds" of that time, since, were he in front of them, they might "shout [him] down" when they disagreed or make him repeat sentences they found "particularly stirring," such were the conditions of performance that prevailed.[10] Even an English visitor to America in

1832, novelist Frances Trollope, bemoaned the Shakespearean audience's "perpetual" noises and the fact that "when a patriotic fit seized them, and 'Yankee Doodle' was called for, every man seemed to think his reputation as a citizen depended on the noise he made."[11]

We need wonder if pejoratives like "rubes" or "yokels," long intended in the USA to demean individuals considered unsophisticated, were to some extent used against individuals who were more orally inclined and who, when they visited the theaters were accustomed—as Levine himself advises—to acting and interacting as participants. They could enter into the action, "feel a sense of immediacy and even of control" of the performance, and unself-consciously "articulate their opinions and feelings vocally and unmistakably."[12] One thing they obviously weren't was tight-lipped!

Notes

1 This appears at line 1067 (56).
2 Foley, *How to Read*, 128.
3 These, and the ensuing words of Kouyaté's, appear in in the chapter "The Words of the Griot," which precedes Niane's translation of *Sundiata*, 1.
4 Johnson, *Epic of Son-Jara*.
5 Ibid., 96. These lines, 2880–2887, appear at the end of episode 6.
6 Naficy, "Theorizing 'Third World,'" 189–190.
7 Shafik, "Egyptian Cinema," 39.
8 Quoted in Ong, *Orality and Literacy*, 21.
9 Ong, *Orality and Literacy*, 66.
10 Levine, *Highbrow/Lowbrow*, 9.
11 Quoted in Levine, *Highbrow/Lowbrow*, 25.
12 Levine, *Highbrow/Lowbrow*, 26.

References

Beowulf. Trans. Burton Raffel. New York: Signet Classic, 1999.
Foley, John Miles. *How to Read an Oral Poem*. Urbana: University of Illinois Press, 2002.

Johnson, John William. *The Epic of Son-Jara: A West African Tradition*. Notes, translation and new introduction by John William Johnson. Text by Fa-Digi Sisòkò. Bloomington: Indiana University Press, 1992.

Levine, Lawrence W. *Highbrow/Lowbrow: The Emergence of Cultural Hierarchy in America*. Cambridge, MA: Harvard University Press, 1988.

Naficy, Hamid. "Theorizing 'Third World' Film Spectatorship." *Rethinking Third Cinema*. Eds. Anthony R. Guneratne and Wimal Dissanayake. New York: Routledge, 2003. 183–201.

Niane, Dijbril Tamsir. *Sundiata: An Epic of Old Mali*. London: Longman, 1965.

Ong, Walter J. *Orality and Literacy: The Technologizing of the Word*. London: Methuen, 1982.

Shafik, Viola. "Egyptian Cinema." *Companion Encyclopedia of Middle Eastern and North African Film*. Ed. Oliver Leaman. London: Routledge, 2001. 23–129.

22 The *agon* of audiences—but, even more, of actors

What choice, colorful word might we use to describe the nature of audiences who, like those patriotic Yankee Doodlers, possess a particular participatory bent? *Argumentative*? Not exactly—they aren't trying to pick a fight. *Bellicose*? No, not quite right either—too negative in shade. *Aggressive*? *Combative*? No, and no—for similar reason. Perhaps it's no accident that to find a word that works, we are best served by pulling from the ancient Greeks. As for that word, it is *agonistic*, which derives from *agon*, the ancient Greek term for a struggle or contest—whether one in athletics, as would have happened at Olympia in the Peloponnese, or in drama, as would have occurred in the great open theaters of Athens.

While you are likely most familiar with *agon* as embedded in the word *agony*, the negative connotation of that latter word is a bit of a modern misnomer. For, while agon is indeed embedded in the word *antagonist*, it is no less so in the word for that antagonist's rival—the *protagonist*. In fact, in the ancient theatrical context, the agon was the contest or rhetorical debate that occurred precisely between these two characters: the *protos* (first) and the *anti* (against). Even more, actors were quite literally *agonistes*, in the sense of their being actors or competitors (hence the derivation of *protagonist* from *protos* + *agonistes*, meaning the first of those who, as an actor, engages in the contest).

As for that contest, it was, in its standard form, a two-sided argument built on opposing principles. That form may be familiar to you either by way of the philosophical dialogues of Plato or ancient Greek plays like Aeschylus' trilogy *Oresteia* or Sophocles' stand-alone *Oedipus Rex*. The term for that staged back-and-forth when in its most stylized form was *stichomythia* and, much as you can glean from the sample of stichomythia below (which I've taken directly from *Oedipus Rex*), its dialogue hinges on a dualistic interplay of thesis-antithesis, question-answer, or argument-refutation. Indeed, because of that, we hardly need any context for this exchange between Oedipus and his brother-in-law, Creon, whom Oedipus suspects of wanting to appropriate his seat of imperial power:

CREON: Now listen to me. You have talked; let me talk too.
            You can not judge unless you know the facts.
OEDIPUS: You speak well: there is one fact; but I find it hard
            To learn from the deadliest enemy I have.
CREON: That above all I must dispute with you.
OEDIPUS: That above all I will not hear you deny.
CREON: If you think there is anything good in being stubborn
            Against all reason, then I say you are wrong.
OEDIPUS: If you think a man can sin against his own kind
            And not be punished for it, I say you are mad.[1]

Of course, the dramatic irony embedded in this passage is that Oedipus *has* sinned against his own kind—something everyone in the ancient Greek audience would have come to the play knowing. (Like Homer's audience then, so, too, were Sophocles' spectators engaging in stories that were decidedly preknown, though playwrights like Sophocles also took artistic and dramaturgical liberties with their material.) Notice how the back and forth here—a kind of internally situated call and response, if you will—produces or elicits a higher level of tension, a more intense emotion, indeed a kind of agony.

So, it's hardly only orally inflected audiences like the Americans responding to Shakespeare or the transnational hecklers of movie screens that reflect agonistic qualities. The same can also be said of actors—and this includes ones who appear in late-twentieth-century Bollywood masala films. In fact, we've already addressed several instances of that heightened display, as in the case of actors

Figure 22.1 Production still for the silent film *Race for Life* (dir. Mack Sennett, 1913). Courtesy of Alamy. The impetus for the melodramatic acting style and sensationalism typical of many American silent films is often attributed to the Vaudeville stage. It's quite possible, though, that both styles owed as much to the greater intelligibility—especially for polyglot immigrant audiences—of oral characteristics of narrative (yes, even in a silent film!). Consider, after all, the films' oft exaggerated acting, their archetypal plot elements (like the damsel-in-distress witnessed here), and their stereotypical characters, complete with epithets, such as this film's "Mabel, Sweet and Lovely" (played by Mabel Normand) and its "Villainous Rival" (played by Ford Sterling), with his "visual epithet" of evil moustache-twirling. The films' draw on the oral episteme certainly rounds out silent-film historian Ben Singer's assertion that their sensationalism was due to the new proletariat viewership being predisposed "toward startling and violent spectacle."[2]

when verbalizing oaths. And why would that be, once more? Because articulating an oath agonistically—as, say while shuddering at the powers inherent in one's declaration to maim, avenge, kill—incarnates the veracity of the words being said.

In fact, the Hindi-film industry cleverly determined ways to *visualize* verbomotor speech. While likely unaware that they were appealing to oral ways of knowing, masala filmmakers nonetheless developed a technical agonism—by way of rapid zooms-in on a protagonist as he verbalizes his pledge, for example, or via a camera circling him with vertiginous speed. Like the sound-effectual wind that might recall a deity's sanction of a hero's planned vengeance, or screeching violins to preordain doom, such technical cues function much like those formulary expressions out of which oral epic's architecture is built. And how swiftly they are able to connote fear, or yearning, or escalating rage, or *Get away now!*—or, just as ably, to project love at first sight. Anyone familiar with Hong Kong's cinema industry, as well as particular breeds of Mexican *telenovelas* or American soap operas, can likely also relate to such instantly messaged technical indicators of how one should feel or what one should think. While painfully overwrought to some viewers, emphatic cinematography and sound effects function as cues that are pragmatically familiar, definitive, and easy to read. Moreover, how better to remember something—especially a scene's momentousness—than through its being etched on your mind in highly exaggerated form?

Notes

1 Sophocles, *Oedipus Rex*, 29. These lines appear in Scene 2.
2 Singer, *Melodrama and Modernity*, 96.

References

Singer, Ben. *Melodrama and Modernity: Early Sensational Cinema and Its Contexts*. New York: Columbia University Press, 2001.
Sophocles. *Oedipus Rex. The Oedipus Cycle: An English Version*. Trans. Dudley Fitts and Robert Fitzgerald. New York: Houghton Mifflin Harcourt, 2002.

23 Blood and guts

Let's pause here to consider your own story-remembering habits as a child. Again, I'm not asking you to focus on these because I want you to associate orality with childlike behavior or, least of all, with a child's level of cognition. Rather, it's that readers today—especially ones with a decades-long immersion in alphabetic literacy under their belt—have often lost connection to what naturally facilitates remembering a story and, so, to how a prelit story might have *had* to be told to safeguard its transmission through time.

Would I be terribly wrong to suppose that at least one overriding thing you remember from then is the *violence*? How about that wolf in "Little Red Riding Hood" eating poor old Grandmother, or Gretel pushing the cannibalistic witch into her own fired-up oven, or Bluebeard's closet hanging with the corpses of his murdered wives? Lest you think these memories are but the residual scars of childhood, check out just a few gorily choice excerpts from the oral epics, which of course, like the original fairy tales, were intended for audiences of all ages. This first one appears in the 16th "book" of the *Iliad*—and, once again, I don't really need to provide any context:

> Idomeneus skewered Erymas straight through the mouth.
> the merciless brazen spearpoint raking through,
> up under the brain to split his glistening skull—

teeth shattered out, both eyes brimmed to the lids
with a gush of blood and both nostrils spurting.
mouth gaping, blowing convulsive sprays of blood
and death's dark cloud closed down around his corpse.[1]

Here's another, from the 68th "book" of the *Mahabharata*, an epic
that, much like the *Iliad*, is centrally figured on a great war.

Drawing his keen-edged sword, and trembling with rage,
[the Pandava prince Bhima] placed his foot upon the throat
of [the Kaurava prince] Dushasana and, ripping open the
breast of his enemy, drank his warm lifeblood little by little.
Then, looking at him with wrathful eyes, he said, "I consider
the taste of this blood superior to that of my mother's milk."[2]

Clearly, agonism isn't exclusive to *verbal* performance in the oral
tradition. True, you may be thinking, and quite appropriately,
that physical violence is to be expected in tales of war, and that
rivals or adversaries in hand-to-hand combat are bound to wreak
havoc. But oral epic has a particular affinity for violence that is
descriptively ripe, ample, and sometimes just a bit too enthusias-
tically gruesome. Moreover, it wields that violence far beyond the
battleground landscapes reflected in the preceding excerpts from
ancient India and ancient Greece.

Take this passage from *Beowulf*—which appears at the point in
"Book" 2 when Grendel, in the darkness of night, sneaks up on
the Danes drunkenly asleep in their mead house:

… The monster's
Thoughts were as quick as his greed or his claws:
He slipped through the door and there in the silence
Snatched up thirty men, smashed them
Unknowing in their beds and ran out with their
     bodies,
The blood dripping behind him, back
To his lair, delighted with his night's slaughter.[3]

Not violent enough? Well, then, how about this from "Book" 11's account of what happens just before Beowulf attacks Grendel and succeeds in dismembering his arm:

> Grendel snatched at the first Geat
> He came to, ripped him apart, cut
> His body to bits with powerful jaws,
> Drank the blood from his veins and bolted
> Him down, hands and feet; death
> And Grendel's teeth came together,
> Snapping life shut.[4]

This willingness to indulge in the outrageously agonistic goes beyond violence, too—into other dark realms of dread and terror. West African epic, for instance, is not the least averse to moving with only the shortest step from "dark humor to tragicomedy," as Isidore Okpewho observes, and, then, from there, "to full-scale horror."[5] Even more, in "a song of terror the bard does not hesitate to make the most of that element without the least intent to amuse anyone."[6] By the way, those more benign fairy tales associated foremost with the Grimm Brothers? Many of them were far more violent and horrifying in pre-bowdlerized form. But my favorite example of late, I have to confess—one that shares something tonally with so many fairy tales—comes from the Viking *Saga of the Volsungs*, which recounts the heroic deeds of Sigurd the Dragon Slayer. This particular episode, however, precedes Sigurd's birth, relating instead what occurs when "King Volsung and his sons journey to Gautland ..." In the relevant scene, an evil she-wolf approaches Sigmund, Sigurd's future father, who is trapped in the stocks, but who has also craftily smeared his face with honey. And, so, upon that she-wolf reaching him:

> She licked his face all over with her tongue and then reached her tongue into his mouth. He did not lose his composure and bit into the wolf's tongue. She jerked and pulled back

hard, thrusting her feet against the trunk [of the stocks] so that it split apart. But Sigmund held on so tightly that the wolf's tongue was torn out by the roots, and that was her death.[7]

True, in noncombat scenarios, such amplification—such *over*amplification, redundant as that may sound (no, wait—precisely because it is redundant!)—may derive from the poet's attempt to reflect other contingencies: the physical struggles endemic to life, the hardships associated with ruling a kingdom. And, yes, it may also be there for the same and arguably ignoble reasons that sensationalized violence is pervasive in today's super-hero movies: because it keeps you, quite literally, on the edge of your seat. Nothing vitalizes human presence like the fear and possibility of losing it. But as Walter J. Ong vigorously maintains, such overamplification in epic also exists because writing did not. Without that proto-external hard drive known as inscription, there is nothing to "disengage knowledge from the arena where human beings struggle with one another."[8] So, when knowledge has to remain grounded in the extant human world, best, and maybe even essential, is to situate it within a literal struggle, within an actual physical give-and-take—which will later get imported and artistically crafted into techniques like stichomythia.

Think of it this way: When all verbal communication has to be accomplished by way of mouth (no pen, no keyboard, no jotting something down, and certainly no looking anything up on Wikipedia), it's probably most efficient to keep that communication dynamic. Style it like a tug of war—and a war housed in highly interpersonal relations: Hera against Zeus; Achilles against Hector; Grendel's Mother against Beowulf; or Gilgamesh battling Enkidu, followed by Gilgamesh *with* Enkidu battling Humbaba. Incidentally, these antagonisms aren't exhibited solely through luridly illustrated acts of violence. Just as vital is the way they can be kept interpersonally high by way of hard-hitting rhetorical devices: name-callings, tongue-lashings, stichomythic taunts—even downright silly taunts, the sort you find in slapstick comedy.

After all, the downright silly, as memory research reveals, is far better recalled than the downright sensible.[9]

Imagine being called a "[b]oastful fool"[10]—as Unferth does Beowulf before going on to malign him for not having been able as a youth to check his pride. Thus will Beowulf, after correcting Unferth's account with his own narration of the mentioned incident (a swimming contest with a friend who, yes, officially did win the race, but only because Beowulf had to do battle with nine sea monsters). And so, now, with his good name fully reestablished, Beowulf will accuse Unferth of the worst of all sins: "[Y]ou murdered your brothers / Your own close kin."[11]

In the Anglo-Saxon tradition, there was even a word for this tradition of trading insults: *flyting*. The word comes from the ancient Old English verb *flitan*, meaning "to quarrel"—which itself comes from the Old Norse *flyta*, for provocation. In later, post literate permutations, flyting would become more aesthetically stylized, whether in early modern court entertainments (with the flyting often sexual or scatological) or, even more recently, in gangsta rap.[12] In its prelit days, however, the emphasis was on a kind of verbal vetting. Most of the flyting in *Beowulf*, for instance—the boasting, the bragging, the challenging of another through words—centers on physical prowess, not on mental agility; indeed, it is the righteousness of Beowulf's moral commitment through his *bodily* competence that is intended to fuel those around him toward their own honorable (and just as physical prowess-oriented) actions.[13] Flyting, in this circumstance, can also operate didactically, particularly as a form of warning. One might need, for instance, verbally to summon the sins or bad deeds of a past foe or, more belligerently, to remind one's contemporary of his scandalous misbehavior—such as in having murdered his brothers, his "own close kin."

Notes

1 Homer, *Iliad*, 423–424. The lines are 407–413 of this 16th "book."
2 *Mahabharata*, 163. These lines are from "Book" LXVIII.
3 This passage appears at lines 119–125 (27).

4 These are lines 739–745 (46).
5 Okpewho, *Epic in Africa*, 208.
6 Ibid.
7 *Saga of the Volsungs*, 41–42.
8 Ong, *Orality and Literacy*, 43.
9 Wolf, *Tales of Literacy*, 14.
10 This is at line 507 (39).
11 This appears at lines 587–589 (41).
12 Halama, "Flytes of Fancy."
13 Ibid., 81.

References

Beowulf. Trans. Burton Raffel. New York: Signet Classic, 1999.

Halama, Alta Cools. "Flytes of Fancy: Boasting and Boasters from Beowulf to Gangsta Rap." *Essays in Medieval Studies* 13 (1996): 81–93.

Homer. *The Iliad*. Trans. Robert Fagles. New York: Penguin Classics, 1998.

The Mahabharata: An English Version Based on Selected Verses. Trans. and ed. Chakravarthi V. Narasimhan. New York: Columbia University Press, 1965.

Okpewho, Isidore. *The Epic in Africa: Toward a Poetics of the Oral Performance*. New York: Columbia University Press, 1979.

Ong, Walter J. *Orality and Literacy: The Technologizing of the Word*. London: Methuen, 1982.

The Saga of the Volsungs: The Norse Epic of Sigurd the Dragon Slayer. Trans. Jesse L. Byock. New York: Penguin Books, 1990.

Wolf, Maryanne, with Stephanie Gottwald. *Tales of Literacy for the 21st Century*. Oxford: Oxford University Press, 2016.

24 Violence + veneration = a polarized world

So, here's one particularly noteworthy dimension to the agonistic transactions that transpire in oral epic: They don't necessarily or exclusively possess a hostile or aggressively assertive edge. They can and do appear just as frequently, and just as vitally, as the polar opposite—which is to say, as an equally excessive expression of *praise*. Walter J. Ong is quite strident when drawing attention to this counterpart to violence in primary epic, noting that effusive approbation is found "everywhere in connection with orality."[1] The praise can come packaged as the lavish tribute paid to a hero or to one's principled sons, or, more broadly, as the ripe glorification of all one's social relations. Rather than vicious, this sort of oral verbalization is venerating, magnanimous. In fact, for those inculcated into an alphabetically literate way of knowing, it often feels excessively ecstatic or cringe-worthily maudlin (or "gushy," in a somewhat less high-minded word).

Sometimes these expressions of praise can be embedded in formulaic epithets. Achilles, for instance, is not only "swift-footed," but also "lion-hearted" and "like to the gods." As for Odysseus, he is not merely "wily" but a "man of many resources," the "great glory of the Achaeans," both a "master mariner" and "mastermind of war." Even when these characters aren't exactly living up to their appellations, they're still referred to by way of these exalting tags. Why? Because the listener understands that the epithets reflect who *ultimately* they are. In the case of *Beowulf*, the Twitter-like handle for its Danish king may be somewhat more lackluster: "Hrothgar, gray-haired and brave." But that certainly doesn't account for his affective disposition. Just listen to how Hrothgar responds in the following passage to Beowulf, who, having recently slain Grendel, is ready now to return home to his native land:

> ... The old king kissed him,
> Held that best of all warriors by the shoulder
> And wept, unable to hold back his tears.
> Gray and wise, he knew how slim
> Were his chances of ever greeting Beowulf
> Again, but seeing his face he was forced
> To hope. His love was too warm to be hidden.
> His tears came running too quickly to be checked ....[2]

So, does the tone of this strike you as admiringly and even indulgently agonistic? Very likely yes, I'm going to guess. Might you even go so far as to consider it melodramatic? Possibly, given that many of us have been culturally trained in the ways of "literately minded" ears and expression. But high and sensational lamentations like these, much like high and sensational violence—and perhaps especially when we jarringly shift from one to the other—aid in making the story memorable. Exaggeration—on both ends—reinforces the retention of knowledge in the oral context. It is hardly a literary flaw or (apologies here) an Achilles heel.

Of course, what this double-sided exaggeration often fosters is a highly polarized world, a storytelling environment built out of affective opposites. That intense brutality in concert with an intense bathos unavoidably induces into other binaries: good versus evil, virtue versus vice, villains versus heroes. In a sense, what gets fashioned is a *narrative* stichomythia. Hence the voluminous amount of ink spilled by philosophers trying to explicate and even rationalize why Achilles in the *Iliad* displays such savagery but is then able to turn immediately to a state of doting amicability—before instantly turning back again to being insulted and enraged. Even Plato wondered and worried about the rival demands placed on the warrior's soul in Homer's oeuvre: Where are we "to find a character that is both gentle and big-tempered [*megalothumon*] at the same time? After all, a gentle nature is the opposite of an angry one."[3] While you will hear all manner of explanation when it comes to these dramatic shifts about honor, about the influence of powerful emotions, and about having to juggle values that are often at loggerheads, one of the less sexy, literary, or complicated reasons for their existence has simply to do with the nature of producing, performing, assimilating, and retaining a narrative by oral means.

When is the last time you heard a work of adult fiction told out loud in agonistic tones both angry *and* acclamatory? I say "adult fiction" because I'm going to guess that the last time you participated in such a vigorous telling was in your youth. Even when we attend public gatherings to hear narrative performed, we're typically listening to writers reading from their latest novel or book of poems, with both the writer (and the writing) comparatively nonaggressive and restrained. That's why, whenever I teach *Beowulf*, I start by reading a few lines out loud with the same vocal agonism and gestural energies that Benjamin Bagby brings to the epic during his concerts. My unabashed railings, my booming protests and melodramatic wails often—no, pretty much *always*—incite student embarrassment, not to mention that they leave even me feeling slightly ridiculous. As alphabetic readers—as trained *silent* readers, even more—our appreciation of verbomotor speech has been massively restricted. We are no longer wed, nor even residually accustomed, to communicating with an ear on the oral economy. Verbomotor speech is consequently more likely to strike us as "insincere, flatulent, and comically pretentious."[4] In fact, I bet most of us when reading *Beowulf* in our typically self-segregated way, probably unconsciously downplay the agonism with which it was originally performed. We lower its decibel range, so to speak, adjusting its volume to our level of narrating text in our head.

If we turn to the twentieth-century hit masala film, however, we find plenty of contemporary evidence for those linked characteristics of agonistic oratory–high violence–high glorification–and resultant polarization. This is especially the case of films produced during the 1980s–1990s, when television led to upscale audiences abandoning the cinema halls, leaving theatrical movie viewing to the lower classes. So, in films from that era, spectators are often set squarely within the sort of tugs-of-war I charted earlier: the blood-and-guts on the one hand, the praise-and-glory on the other (with the latter often most richly vitalized through song and dance). I cannot stress enough the presence—the omnipresence—in these movies of displays of agonistic oratory–high violence–high glorification–and resultant polarization. True, they manifest in ways far more domestic than what you'll find in an epic like the *Iliad*, with its years-long war and dozens of armed ships crowding the sea adjacent to Troy. But they also unself-consciously provide us, say, a beefy underworld gangster being fed by his doting mother, after having just jujutsu-ed his way through twelve goons wielding daggers. Don't be surprised either to find him participating in some very charged rituals of romantic bonding—before taking a very charged revolver to a nemesis' head. (The movie I'm citing here is 1993's *Khal Nayak*, which literally translates as "Villain.") While the masala film may be cruder than Homer's lofty songs in its presentation of these tributes and hostilities, the outcome is the same: a highly polarized world in which actions deemed honorable, noble, pure, or chaste will be gloriously overstated in terms of their ethical and spiritual allure, just as evil will ultimately be ingloriously derided for its repellence.

Notes

1 Ong, *Orality and Literacy*, 44.
2 This passage appears at lines 1870–1877 (81).
3 Quoted in Reeve, "Anger of Achilles." The bracketed portion is in the original.
4 Ong, *Orality and Literacy*, 45.

References

Beowulf. Trans. Burton Raffel. New York: Signet Classic, 1999.

Ong, Walter J. *Orality and Literacy: The Technologizing of the Word.* London: Methuen, 1982.

Reeve, C.D.C. "The Anger of Achilles." *Aeon.com.* Retrieved July 20, 2019, from https://aeon.co/essays/the-anger-that-fuels-homers-hero-is-both-honourable-and-divine.

25 When exteriority is not a bad thing

So, if agonism in the form of both violence *and* fawning adulation in lengthy oral poems seems curious, here's something more: It's hardly exclusive to those realms. In fact, one could argue that all emotions in primary epic are staged in ways that are outwardly directed and externally motivated. That's because emotions in these narratives aren't intended as evidence of private feelings that are psychologically one's own. Their purpose instead is to reflect and prop up *social* relations. Consequently, shame, not guilt, is the overriding dread of epic warriors—no matter whether we're talking about Gilgamesh, or Achilles, or even, much later, the medieval knight Roland (of the Old French epic *Song of Roland*). Shame, after all, inherently relies on others to initiate or keep a warrior (or a lover even) in that agonized state. Once upon a time, we even had a word for it in English: *beshaming*. (Perhaps the more public communication environment of Twitter—complete with its own text-based permutation of flyting—will revitalize that word in the years to come, maybe even generating a flurry of activity for the [already extant] hashtag "#beshamed.") Even Shakespeare's oeuvre references shame far more often than it ever does guilt. Honor, by the way, operates in much the same capacity in primary epic—in that it is not something intrinsic to, or lacking from, one's internal sense of being but, rather, a virtue fundamentally bestowed by others.

We might even propose (rather boldly, admittedly) that, in the oral environment, attempts to parse oneself in a manner disconnected from the group would make one seem less human, not more. Of course, what, then, would that say of our contemporary appetite for inspecting our own inner psyches, or of desiring access—as, for example, through literature and film—to the so-called interior lives of characters? Could these latter proclivities say no more about our actually accessing something more psychologically "authentic" about ourselves than they do about our having receded further (and further) away from the public pressures of the oral tradition, from the expectation that our states be expressed in communal terms?

Grief, which many of us today construe as a private emotion, as something generally kept internally cloistered, is executed in the epical tradition with particular vociferousness. Perhaps nowhere is its outward display better exemplified than in "book" eighteen of the *Iliad*, when Achilles learns of his companion Patroclus' death:

> A black cloud of grief came shrouding over Achilles.
> Both hands clawing the ground for soot and filth,
> he poured it over his head, fouled his handsome face
> and the black ashes settled onto his fresh clean war-shirt.
> Overpowered in all his power, sprawled in the dust,
> Achilles lay there, fallen …
> tearing his hair, defiling it with his own hands.[1]

So shrilly does Achilles scream after this dramatization of his mourning that his mother, "silver-footed" Thetis, descends from her celestial realm to console him. True, today's intellectual might justifiably interpret Achilles' befouling of himself with grime and soot as evidence of his desire for his outward appearance to match his inner state. But would that inner state have been sufficient—indeed, would it have been there at all—were it not for Achilles' public disfiguration of his outward appearance?

Gilgamesh's grief over the death of his friend Enkidu is likewise ripe and acutely oriented toward others: "Hear me, O Elders of Uruk, hear me, O men! / I mourn for Enkidu, my friend. / I shriek in anguish like a mourner."[2] Incidentally, in both the Sumerian and the ancient Greek traditions, professional mourners would wail and beat their breasts to reflect and orally emphasize this grief. My own Hindu grandmother did the same, in fact, at the public lamentation held in honor of her husband who died soon after Partition (when in 1947, to reprise, India and Pakistan became independent nations).

For those today whose expressions of deep emotion have gone inward—have been, quite literally, privatized—would such yowls and gesticulations result in some helpless grimacing and heavy cringing? Yes, very possibly. In fact, Englishman Charles Lamb was aghast to find that in the popular theaters of nineteenth-century America, where oral customs could still remain comparatively intact, Hamlet's own inner musings were being "represented by a gesticulating actor, who comes and mouths them out before an audience, making four hundred people his confidants at once."[3] Of course, given that Shakespeare's own world had been "enshrined in the art of oratory," as Lawrence Levine notes,[4] wouldn't that have made Hamlet's paralingual gesturing and direct conferral with his audience more in keeping with the Bard's lived culture rather than anomalous or obtrusive? Not according to Lamb. He went so far as to insist that Shakespeare's oeuvre should not even be permitted performance on the stage, especially when it came to those spectators who comprised the vulgar "multitudes." Shakespeare's plays were "so deep," he argued, "that the depth of them lies out of the reach of most of us."[5] So, was Lamb trying to *de*-melodramatize the Bard's works? Even more, were his aspirations bred by—and even culturally permissible because of—the schooled classes' capacity now to read Shakespeare on the (static, eye-oriented, oratorically suppressed) page?

By no means am I asserting that Shakespeare's works are paradigmatically oral. In fact, in the sequel to this book, I will tackle Shakespeare's positioning vis-à-vis alphabetic literacy in much greater and more nuanced fashion. Suffice it to say for now, though, that while good writing may have been the most effective cognitive scaffold in the production of Elizabethan literature, as Evelyn Tribble proposes, mnemonic devices and the art of rhetoric were central to early modern education, with grammar-school boys receiving "endless training in verbatim memory."[6] So, again, we see evidence of the fascinating interplay that existed at the time—and that continues to exist *through* time—between orality and alphabetic literacy.

In fact, let's move closer to our times: Would you be surprised to learn that melodrama—a genre or type of performance that intentionally sensationalizes events and emotions—has been the characteristic form of storytelling operative in societies undergoing the transition to modernity[7]? And we need hardly limit ourselves to late twentieth-century Bollywood. Just as easily, we can turn to Mexico and its 1990s *telenovelas*, or television serials, which, as Ana M. Lopez observes, likewise pivot on melodrama. They are, as she says, "notorious for their weepiness," as well as for their "extraordinarily Manichean [black-and-white] vision of the world."[8] If constituents of today's reading population find such a vision too simple or naïve, too soap-operatically binary, that may be because they have willingly forfeited our human propensity—our naturally born propensity, according to psychologist Paul Bloom—for dualism.[9] No wonder, thus, that one of the structuring principles of oral narrative—here I'm pulling from Chao Gejin, a folklorist steeped in Mongolian epic—is that of binary opposition precisely.[10] And the same, of course, goes for the masala movies of the last century, where histrionic black-and-whiteness indeed prevails, such that fathers can be found slapping the suitors of their daughters not once but (a melodramatic) eight times; and a broken son in pursuit of redemption can drag himself into his mother's arms, intoning her name "Ma" not eight but a whopping 22 times.

If there's something seemingly *anti*psychological to these narrative displays, there is good, oral rationale for that—and it's definitely *not* because oral individuals are not self-aware. Rather, writing permits both the storyteller and story reader an exceptional divorce from the group, consequently enabling their capacity for heightened introspection and interiority. Burrowing evermore into one's own psyche, in other words, requires a willing self-alienation from the acoustical environment so integral to communication in oral cultures, as well as from those personal loyalties to one's kin or one's tribe which demand social prioritization. (Recall that Wanderer whom earlier we discussed.) No wonder, then, that the producers of those masala films I described above openly associated their movies' intense emotionality with that found in the *Mahabharata*. Like that great Indian epic of princely cousins pitted in battle against each other, their films similarly traffick in amplified demonstrations of sacrifice and revenge, of virulent hate and amorous pining[11]—and, so, possess the higher and more melodramatic pitch identified with myth. They are bolder, louder—and not only acoustically but visually, too (we'll come back to this last attribute momentarily).

To be sure, melodrama, like any of the other characteristics I've outlined so far, is hardly restricted to the oral domain. In fact, in our increasingly "literized" world, the reticulate or constellated characteristics that comprise the oral episteme are often teased away, extracted, and aesthetically played with. But in the context of primary epics that have to pass through the generations by way of traditional bards, melodrama purposely and purposefully operates in—and *as*—language governed by oral principles. In the oral milieu, therefore, melodrama is necessarily exoteric. The poet's language, like the characters he portrays or the plot in which he entangles them, retains an outward orientation. Rarely is anything "hidden" in the narrative that requires private deciphering; seldom is the poet carrying something—pardon the cliche—up his sleeve. Why? Because, ultimately, his words, their meaning, and his stories more broadly are intended to be intelligible and understood by all. They are flat and diagrammatic; they arrive already interpreted, in a manner of speaking. They cannot afford to be indirect or abstruse, or to possess undertones or subtleties that would endanger meaning's transmission. Hence their propensity toward heightened antagonisms *and* heightened friendships—and heightened shame, compounded by heightened attempts to reclaim honor. This is likely why the heroic grandeur they project is always a "two-edged sword, sublime and terrible."[12] Philosopher C.D.C. Reeve was here describing Achilles, but the line applies no less to that masala-film protagonist who pummeled a dozen thugs with bloodthirsty vengeance and then cried out "Ma" 22 times in the hopes of garnering mercy and maternal benediction.

Think how compromised the knowledge embedded in oral epics would become were its poet to incorporate or make regular use of devices that were not, shall we say, epistemologically frontal (which is just my fancy way of saying "in your face"). Think what you would be imperiling were you to communicate your story using veiled, undeclared, or even "secret" symbolism, that mandates that listeners had independently to mine for the untold meaning of X (in other words, X is not only X, but also signifying Y). Or, imagine your story indulging in what you inventively, or even obstinately, *refuse* to say, such as in a novel like Thomas Mann's *The Magic Mountain*, where untold meaning "lurk[s] almost pathologically between the lines"[13] (and so, *is* there a Y, and how can I know for certain Mann's not making Y up?).

Now, translate this requirement and expectation of epistemological frontality to the milieu of a movie. If a feature film were being designed, whether purposely or unconsciously, for an intrinsically oral body of spectators, do you suppose those spectators would appreciate a film rife with unremitting symbolism that is never explained? Or how about long gaps in which nothing appears to be happening because the meaning is veiled (and, so, would there even be an X in their mind—which is to say, would there even be a *story* playing out on the screen)? These latter sorts of narrative features demand, after all, that audiences detach themselves from the words that the poet, whether actual or ersatz, is uttering; that they step away from the very knowledge that is being communicated—and *ephemerally* communicated for the oral spectator, recall. In the context of a live performance, once spoken, those words are gone, gone, gone, and they cannot be retrieved for the sake of interpretation or a mulling-over—not unless a listener has the audacity to stop the song! Symbolism, indefinite meaning, cageyness, tacit or unspoken meaning: All these render a text, to borrow Blakey Vermeule's keen phrasing, "[h]ighly Machiavellian"[14]—which is to say, more calculatedly complex in a way that puts intentional interpretive stress on a reader (and here I'm intentionally highlighting the *reader*).

Okay, so some of you may remain unconvinced or skeptical still. Perhaps you had a brilliant instructor who devoted an entire class period to symbolism in the *Iliad* (the ships! the shield!) or no less to its presence in *Gilgamesh* (the bull! the snake!). Let me clarify, then, that when I refer to symbols, it's to distinguish them from *totems*. You're no doubt familiar with the latter term in relation to the North American totem pole, which is composed of carved figures, often animals, that indicate kinship groups. But the word, which derives from the Ojibwe language, has also been imported into disciplines like psychoanalysis and literature to more generally reflect a revered emblem or sacred representation—with words like "revered" and "sacred" hinting not only at the totem's spiritual significance, but also to the fact that this object would have been entirely *familiar* to its family, clan, or tribe. In other words, totems in this context, unlike symbols, are always already shared and preknown. They are transparent visual tropes whose emotively rousing or ritualized meanings don't require independent translation. What are some of the best examples of totems in our own time? Think the Christian cross (for Christians, at least), the White House (for Americans), the Kaaba at Mecca (for Muslims), the military uniform (as distinct from the suit and tie, or wedding dress, or priest's cassock), and just about everyone's own communal flag or national anthem. This particular category of tropes need not be positive in sentiment either. No less charged are totems like the swastika or the KKK hood—or in some circumstances, arguably, the totem pole when fashioned into a hollowed-out emblem plastered onto touristy t-shirts.

In the context of oral epic, characters came invested with totemic power even in advance of a poet's performance of their story, given that they themselves were preknown—proto-Hollywood "stars" of sorts. And in the case of the stars of 1970s–1990s Bollywood, they sometimes carry with them from one movie to the next the physical totems responsible for their preknown power—a violin, say, which at some point they will play; spectacles; a cane; a certain fashion sense. Scholars of the Roman Catholic religion might be more prone to calling these *attributes*. Attributes were especially important in medieval times in the identification of the saints. Few folks could read, after all, and, so, required visual aids to help them differentiate the hundreds of holy personages dotting the cultural landscape, as well as to facilitate recollection of those saints' stories. Thus do we find St. Francis recurrently depicted in his monastic brown robe with his palms marked by stigmata wounds, and St. Catherine carting around the spiked wheel on which she was brutally tortured to death.

Perhaps all this is starting to sound like I'm pushing the stuff of formula. If so, well, then, frankly, I'm doing my job! But don't be fooled: In spite of my providing you what on the surface may appear prescriptive—like some kind of uncomplicated how-to recipe for the production of an episodic–formulaic–unoriginal–exoteric–black and white oral epic—I'm going to guess that you (like me) would fail consistently at producing a sophisticated one of your own. So, perhaps we're better off asking when it was that formula became such a dirty word. Its modern use as a descriptor for narrative is customarily intended as a means of disparaging a work. Far less often does one hear, "That writer has got the detective formula down" than "That detective novel [or film, or TV series, or game] is so dreadfully formulaic." When originally imported into English in the 1630s, the Latin *formula* (literally "small form") signified a pattern of fixed words often used in a ceremony or ritual. *Formular*, however, was already in use—representative, since the 1560s, of a model or exemplar. It's quite a bit later, in 1845 in fact, that an -ic was finally affixed to the original Latin word to produce the adjectival *formulaic*. Alas, by then, Thomas Carlyle had already queered the semantic pitch, having in 1837 equated formula with a "rule slavishly followed without understanding."[15]

Contemporary medieval musician Benjamin Bagby might argue—this I'm basing on the short interviews he provides on his *Beowulf* performance DVD—that the real slavishness resides in our modern commitment to the written word. We believe in, and even unwittingly fetishize, the false fixity of an oral poem like Beowulf, treating it like a single, original, inelastic work that resides rigidly and undeviatingly on the page. That sort of relationship Bagby appears to find artificially constricting, preferring instead the freedom and flexibility of being able to rearrange themes and formulae—which was, of course, what storytellers *had* to do in preliterate times. How else for a poet to juggle his vast mental storehouse of information, along with the requirements that he appeal to a variety of contexts, including audience expectations? Besides, oral poets are hardly in a position—nor would they probably think it virtuous or signal of their aesthetic superiority were they to try—to produce the entire compass of a work out of their own being.

Notes

1 Homer, *Iliad*, 468. The lines are 25–30 of this 18th "book."
2 *Epic of Gilgamesh*. The excerpt is from Tablet IX.
3 Quoted in Levine, *Highbrow/Lowbrow*, 73.
4 Levine, *Highbrow/Lowbrow*, 36.
5 Quoted in Levine, *Highbrow/Lowbrow*, 73.
6 Tribble, "Distributing Cognition," 152.
7 Vasudevan, *Melodramatic Public*, 105.
8 Lopez, "Our Welcomed Guests," 261–262.
9 Vermeule, *Why Do We Care*, 24.
10 Gejin, "Mongolian Oral Epic," 334.
11 Bollywood screenwriter Anjum Rajabali, in Ganti, *Bollywood*, 183.
12 Reeve, "Anger of Achilles."
13 Vermeule, *Why Do We Care*, 90.
14 Ibid., 106.
15 This quote comes from www.etymonline.com, by way of the *Oxford English Dictionary*. You can retrieve it via www.etymonline.com/word/formula#etymonline_v_11816.

References

The Epic of Gilgamesh. Trans. Maureen Gallery Kovacs. Electronic edition by Wolf Carnahan, 1998. Academy of Ancient Texts. Retrieved

August 8, 2017, from www.ancienttexts.org/ library/Mesopotamian/ gilgamesh.

Ganti, Tejaswini. *Bollywood: A Guide Book to Popular Hindi Cinema.* New York: Routledge, 2004.

Gejin, Chao. "Mongolian Oral Epic: An Overview." *Oral Tradition* 12, 2 (1997): 322–336.

Homer. *The Iliad.* Trans. Robert Fagles. New York: Penguin Classics, 1998.

Levine, Lawrence W. *Highbrow/Lowbrow: The Emergence of Cultural Hierarchy in America.* Cambridge, MA: Harvard University Press, 1988.

Lopez, Ana M. "Our Welcomed Guests." *To Be Continued …: Soap Operas Around the World.* Ed. Robert C. Allen. London: Routledge, 1995. 256–275.

Reeve, C.D.C. "The Anger of Achilles." *Aeon.com.* Retrieved July 20, 2019, from https://aeon.co/essays/the-anger-that-fuels-homers-hero-is-both-honourable-and-divine.

Tribble, Evelyn. "Distributing Cognition in the Globe." *Shakespeare Quarterly* 56, 2 (2005): 135–155.

Vasudevan, Ravi. *The Melodramatic Public: Film Form and Spectatorship in Indian Cinema.* New York: Palgrave Macmillan, 2011.

Vermeule, Blakey. *Why Do We Care about Literary Characters?* Baltimore: Johns Hopkins University Press, 2010.

26 But, what of art? What of aesthetics?

Detachment, distance, segregation: These are words I've repeated now several times, and I've done so in in the hopes of conveying how *un*anticipated they are in oral narrative, if not downright intentionally and necessarily preempted. Yes, today we can muse for hours over a passage in Homer or analyze a character from Norse saga down to increasingly tinier and more abstracting bits. But this capacity and even relish to probe, parse, and dissect lengthy narrative as if we were lab technicians is thoroughly a derivative of what *writing* permits us.

As for those words—detachment, distance, and segregation— they are paramount to Enlightenment philosopher Immanuel Kant's notion of what is crucial to the human capacity to appreciate beauty, indeed to judge a work *aesthetically*, by which he means to judge it with "taste." In *Critique of Judgment*, Kant outlines four key criteria that he deems essential to discerning that a landscape (or a painted landscape, or statue or poem) is beautiful: (1) "disinterestedness," meaning that the pleasure comes from the object's beauty, not the other way around (in other words, this is not the beauty of a really, really satisfying looking cheeseburger to your hungry eyes, but an appreciation of an object *without* desire); (2) "universal communicability," meaning that others agree with you about that beauty—disinterestedly, of course (which they probably wouldn't about that cheeseburger if they'd just eaten lunch); (3) "merely formal purposiveness," meaning that the object strikes you, and is intended to strike you, as having no final purpose or utility other than for you to experience and appreciate the formal components of its representation (so forget that cheeseburger); and, finally, (4) the "necessary," meaning that—well, here, to be frank, Kant always loses me (but I think what he'd say about that cheeseburger was that it did not pass the beauty test, according to principle).[1] Fortunately, it's Kant's first criterion which is of real consequence here. For, what "pure disinterestedness satisfaction" requires of us is a kind of standing back: a necessary detachment from an object as a thing of utility or purpose, in order that we might appreciate its formal elements (its texture, tone, form, and so forth).

Although I hardly want, or would ever even deign, to suggest that oral communities cannot appreciate the beautiful, what constitutes beauty, what makes something aesthetically pleasing, cannot but be markedly different in their epistemic milieu. Should we, in fact, anticipate based on all we've covered thus far that, for them, aesthetic judgment might be conceptually grounded in, and even mandate, an object's utility or purpose? Consider especially objects one devoted to carrying forward their history, such as glyphs, or those Rajasthani paintings on cloth, or, or Old Germanic runes. In fact, the word *aesthetics* as we employ it today—notwithstanding its derivation from the Greek word for "perceiving" or for "perceived things"—is really a creation of eighteenth-century Europe.

The notion of "art for art's sake" is likewise a relatively new concept in the history of human culture. Even more recent has been the growing notion of "kitsch for kitsch's sake"—which is to say, the admiration or pleasure taken in an object precisely because that object is considered artistically vulgar by the standards of the day (think porcelain angel figurines, Big-Eye velvet paintings, *Dogs Playing Poker*, and, yes, even Warner Sallman's porcelain-skinned, big-eyed *Head of Christ*). Like aesthetic judgment, this sort of judgment hinges on your conscious recognition through necessary detachment that something qualifies *as* kitsch. So, you are expected to recognize, with a kind of enlightened wink-wink, the object's garish qualities, its sentimental nature, and its shoddy mechanical replication of "genuine culture," as art critic Clement Greenberg would have it.[2] What you are not supposed to do is fall prey to those qualities. Take another look at that poster for the Bollywood blockbuster *Deewar*, which appears in Chapter 2. Would you consider it genuine art or kitsch—and, just as vitally, on what bases of judgment?

Perhaps another example pulled from my own experience will help to capture the colorful complexities of kitsch when it comes to appeal—as well as return us to our broader theme of how that appeal might be animated by epistemic pressures or expectations related to orality and alphabetic literacy. What follows is a description of a scene from a Hindu mythological movie entitled *Hanuman Vijay!* (1974). I saw this "fantasy film" (as Wikipedia terms it) in a theater in New Delhi when I was a child. *Hanuman Vijay!* draws its inspiration from the story of the gods Rama and Sita as told in the originally oral epic the *Ramayana*. Here, though, the emphasis is on the character of the monkey-god Hanuman. One of the most beloved of Hindu deities, especially by those who prize duty as a virtue, Hanuman is famous for retrieving the abducted Sita from the island of Lanka and burning down that evil empire with his alighted tail. As for the origins of the description that follows: It served as the opening for that book I wrote on the cinema and the sacred. There, I argue that themes of religion and spirituality on film, as well as experiences of the numinous through film, need to be understood in the context of—yes, you guessed it—orality and alphabetic literacy. So, here's the scene and, should you want to judge the authenticity or exaggeration of the kitschiness I project, you can do by viewing "Ram Hai Unka Naam" (literally, Ram is his name) for yourself on YouTube:

Picture Sita (or, rather, the movie star playing that Hindu goddess) resplendent in pink and rushing to the window of her artificially ornate palace. As she gazes out from curtains that perfectly match her outfit, we hear Mohammed Rafi on the soundtrack, movingly singing a devotional song about searching for Rama. Cut to a shot of what Sita sees out the window: it is Rama, her husband, and his brother, Laxman, perched on the shoulders of the monkey-god Hanuman. Nebulously they hover in the night sky, the brothers' yellow *salwar* pants fluorescently glowing, before awkwardly Hanuman "flies off." Sita returns to her palatial chambers in order to pay rapturous homage to Rama's statue. As she offers him daisy heads, we get close-ups of her face: her lips trembling in a smile, her eyes adorned with glitter and ecstatically alight. During her fervent devotional display—indeed, one could say rightly *because* of it—Rama's face magically appears, superimposed in those dozen daisies' florets; in the lambent flame of a *deepak*; even in the pupils of Sita's own eyes. And again: in a spinning golden sun—in a paper moon—and, when Sita opens her hands, her palms ornately hennaed with his name, there again Rama's face appears.[3]

So, I'm hoping that you really did visit YouTube to view the clip—and if not, go now, before you read another word!

Notes

1 This is a distillation of his chapter "Analytic of the Beautiful," 3–40.
2 Greenberg, "Avant-Garde and Kitsch," 10.
3 Nayar, *Sacred and the Cinema*, 1.

References

Greenberg, Clement. "Avant-Garde and Kitsch." *Art and Culture: Critical Essays*. Boston: Beacon Press, 1989.

Kant, Immanuel. *Critique of Judgment*. Trans. J.H. Bernard. New York: Barnes & Noble, 2005.

Nayar, Sheila J. *The Sacred and the Cinema: Reconfiguring the Genuinely Religious Film*. New York: Bloomsbury, 2009.

27 Oral embodiment

So, now (at least in my imagination), you are returning to *Before Literature* with visions of plaster deities and daisies dancing in your head—and in anticipation, perhaps, of some sort of debriefing. In accounting for this scene from *Hanuman Vijay!*, we definitely need to make space for the way its technical primitiveness shapes some of that shoddiness to which Clement Greenberg refers. This is especially the case given our present-day, digitally influenced eyes. Nothing makes a movie appear outdated or substandard quite like the conspicuous archaism of its mechanics. On the other hand, more sophisticated technical elements don't rule out or negate the possibility of oral inflection. (Remember my earlier citing of the Hollywood blockbuster *Titanic*? And let's not forget so many of the comic-book franchise movies that are popular these days.) The thing is, I saw *Hanuman Vijay!* in the company of my grandmother, who prayed whenever that monkey-god appeared on the screen and vocally offered mantras when he accomplished some great feat. I was fascinated by her response—and had we been in a major theater in my hometown of Montreal, no doubt I would have also been highly embarrassed.

It's not that I was cleverer than her—not by any means. So, at the time, I really understand what, beyond cultural heritage, might have accounted for our different responses. Only now, decades later, am able to see that my "Western" schooling was already inculcating me into an alphabetically bound way of nego- tiating and reading the world of the humanities. And according to that latter worldview—which would only strengthen and even harden the further my education on how to read literature and the arts got—over-the-top-ness was an offense, not a way of ensuring that a movie might be more readily enlisted to one's mind. The surface was something you were meant to penetrate; you weren't supposed to be seized by it—unless, of course, you were being seized in a disinterested fashion, such that your capacities to analyze its formal components were being summoned. By "educated" standards, my grandmother was an unsophisticated consumer of the culture industry, while I was in the throes of being trained *out* of being one of those submissive, naïve, or passive folk said to constitute the masses. But therein lies a possible myopia of the educated (as is the potential with any group): The world is judged through the lens of their own making.

See, in the epistemically oral context, the color that seeped through *Hanuman Vijay!*—not only in the sense of its bold technicolo but its outwardly oriented emotive color, too—was precisely what made the film enlistable to the memory. Its textural intensity, apparency, and obviousness, compounded by its presentation of a world semantically black and white (even when in color), were far from draining the movie of its fertility; in fact, they were fundamentally *giving it life*. (That today we privilege classical statuary in undefiled marble form—which is to say, *not* as painted in the bright and even gaudy colors that the effigies actually were [just google "painted ancient Greek statues" to see what I mean]—is symbolic testament to how the past often gets reworked in the image of the educated.) So, we should probably bear in mind that the artificially ornate palace serving as the heroine-goddess Sita's residence in *Hanuman Vijay!*—complete with marble sculpted pillars, gold filigree, and silk curtains—is no less exaggerated and extravagant than are the palaces famously described in the *Mahabharata*.

True, contemporary critics often interpret cinematic utopian abundance as an unintended comment on the privation of the films' audiences. That is, spectators achieve pleasure from viewing and participating in what they existentially lack—namely, material abundance—which producers are willing to provide them in spades. Those producers' primary objective is to reap hefty profits, after all. True, many strains of Hinduism, material display before one's gods is commensurate with the ceremonial respect and adoration being shown those divinities. But just as consequential may be a prelit stimulus, given classicist Eric Havelock's observation that ancient Greek oral epics likewise "glory in conspicuous consumption."[1] What better way to reinforce a spell over one's listeners than by making the story visually spectacular, replete with palatial homes, or thousands of ships, or marvelously crafted shields, swords, crowns, and more? A palace belonging to ancient Kaurava royalty (or the sprawling marble mansion inhabited by our movie Sita) is certainly more impressively memorable than would be a laborer's meager hut in a slum—unless, of course, the latter were no less aggrandized (and stereotyped), in which case it would become The Laborer's Hut, or the quintessence of Slum—which is to say, a totemic embodiment of Hut-ness or Slum-ness. Incidentally, in *The City of* Djinns: A Year in Delhi, William Dalrymple recounts his visit to an archaeological said to be coterminous with the events in the *Mahabharata*. Alas, no palaces turned up, merely mud huts[2]—and ones apparently quite lacking in Hut-ness.

If lavish display can greedily appeal to a body of listeners bereft of material resources, in the oral circumstance, those resources can also serve as handy storage devices, as verbal formulae in *ocular* form. Anyone who has read the *Iliad* surely recalls Homer's description in "Book" 18 of the intricate scene hammered into Achilles' shield by that god of the forge, Hephaestus (Vulcan). Why we remember that scene, though, is likely not for the same reasons that Homer's listeners would have. For many of us today, the shield's memorability derives from our growing awareness as we read of the absolute (and even laughable) impossibility of its illustrating with as much detail and intricacy what Homer claims: earth, heavens, ocean; cities at war and also at peace; pomp, a solemn dance, a hymeneal rite; brides, nuptial beds, youthful dancers; court cases, secret ambushes, ploughmen; wheat fields, vineyards; more comely youths and maidens .... Need I go on? But what better, more effective, more economical means by which to reflect on the cosmos or to stockpile accounts of antiquity? The material object here is not a work of art in the modern sense, one we are supposed to appreciate foremost for its aesthetic value: as a fine example of metallurgical craftsmanship, for instance, or, equally finely, of ekphrasis. (Ekphrasis is a verbal description of a work of art in poetry or literature—so, a lexically crafted shield, in this case.)

Similar sorts of indulgences in conspicuous consumption can be found in *Beowulf*, often in the standard Anglo-Saxon form of glorified gifts. To be sure, vividly particularized gifts can also function as tokens of interpersonal relations, not just as mere eye candy. Even more, they can operate, and quite essentially and evocatively, as history lodged by necessity inside *things*. Consider, for instance, what we learn when, after his defeat of Grendel, Beowulf is gifted "the most beautiful necklace known to men."

> Nowhere in any treasure-hoard anywhere
> On earth was anything like it, not since
> Hama carried the Brosings' necklace
> Home to his glorious city, saved
> Its tight-carved jewels, and his skin, and his soul
> From Ermric's treachery, and then came to God.
> Higlac had it next, Swerting's
> Grandson; defending the golden hoard
> His battle-hard hands had won from him, the Geats'
> Proud king lost it, was carried away
> By fate when too much pride made him feud
> With the Frisians.[3]

Here, the material object is quite explicitly made the carrier of the Germanic past. The same will occur later, when Wiglaf, upon deciding he will join the aged Beowulf in battling the treasure-hoarding dragon, draws his sword. For, upon his doing so, immediately we are cast for several dozen "lines" of verse into the history of the ownership and adventure commemoratively embedded in that "ancient / Weapon that had once belonged to Onela's / Nephew, and that Wexstan had won"—and that Wexstan would keep for many years until he died, after which Wiglaf would become "his heir, inherit[ing] treasures / And weapons and land ...."[4]

You'd be right to suppose that the inspiration for refrains like these might derive from the rarity of such sumptuous objects, ones so valuable and precious they would of course be passed down for generations. Actually, in this way, they make the perfect vehicles for cataloging a generational line and, more traumatically, that line's potential seizure through warfare and plunder. Given the corporate-capitalist brand of conspicuous consumption that we practice today—one built out of disposability and planned obsolescence—we are far less likely to encounter a material thing with such a long and regal provenance. Consequently, it may be difficult for us when reading an oral epic to intuit or grasp the psychological power and sacred depth of a thing's existence. What is more, the history tied *to* that thing would have been neither short nor nostalgic (as is more likely the case with a family heirloom, for instance). After all, these things—the necklaces, the sword hilts—might be serving as the centuries-long antecedents not only to those medieval chronicles eventually written down by hand on parchment, but to today's history books now publishable en masse. As a result, objects in the oral epics might have also evoked a cyclical passing of the torch (and so too, potentially, the passage of time). They might even have cognitively conjured the veritable impermanence of proprietorship—as, say, Wiglaf's "inherited treasures and weapons and land." In fact, could the necessarily intergenerational aspect of *Beowulf* and the like be one of the reasons these stories so often echo with the theme of a hero's inescapable destiny, with death always lurking like a pall?

Notes

1 Havelock, *Greek Concept*, 94.
2 Dalrymple, *City of Djinns*, 321–322.
3 These are lines 1196–1207 (61).
4 These lines run between 2610–2625 (104).

References

Beowulf. Trans. Burton Raffel. New York: Signet Classic, 1999.

Dalrymple, William. *City of Djinns: A Year in Delhi.* New York: Penguin, 1993.

Havelock, Eric A. *The Greek Concept of Justice: From Its Shadow in Homer to Its Substance in Plato.* Cambridge, MA: Harvard University Press, 1978.

28 Superhuman vessels

For those of you new to mining a text like the *Iliad* for its oral properties, my claims of its relative accessibility may appear a hard and unjust pill to swallow—and for understandable reason. We are, after all, removed from that Homeric text by several thousand years. As for why I'm referring to it here as a text: That's because the *Iliad*, which belonged to many a poet other than Homer, has since become immobilized for us exclusively as his. So, while new translations are continuously solicited to amend earlier departures from Homer's spirit or language, or to correct errata, or to render the *Iliad's* language more suitable for our modern ears, its story as structurally recounted does not change, much as it would have with each of its oral poets' renderings. Indeed, that wooden Trojan horse, with the 40 or so Achaeans hiding in its belly and awaiting nightfall in order to besiege Troy, could well have made an appearance in Homer's next-recounted version of the *Iliad*, instead of its now being eternally affixed as a flashback sequence to the *Odyssey*.

Today, we preserve texts; we archive them scrupulously and assign them dates of origin. In a sense, we want to fix them (and everything!) in time. Oral epic, on the other hand, was by its very nature fluid and shape-shifting: vulnerable to (or vitalized by, as the case may be) influences of mood, and audience, and the poet's imaginative state, not to mention its migration through different geographical regions where people might have a some-what different code of ethics or political bent. What would the

Iliad have been, in fact—how different would the story have become—had it continued to pass exclusively by way of oral means all the way down to the twenty-first century? How might those men-at-arms or white-armed Hera have transmuted were the *Iliad* still, to this day, being composed anew with every performance? There is something strangely liberating, I think, in asking and hypothetically answering questions like these; in getting out from under our stringent treatment of Homeric narrative as inert and inflexible—as if the epic were a prisoner of narrative rather than "open-sourced" and in possession of the protean potentials of, say, a Wikipedia page.

Still, to release oral epic respectfully from these strictures, we ought to attend to the last few of those highly resilient characteristics of narrative that stem from orality. In fact, here's one that's part and parcel of virtually every one of its epistemic descendants: characters who are enlarged, amplified, overstated, and larger than life (and, yes, I'm being intentionally superfluous!). Perhaps you've already correctly gleaned that rhetorical flatulence for the sake of making a hero's words mentally stick might predispose him toward being larger than life. If his oaths need to be vigorous, delivered as if from a rostrum facing thousands of people; if both his antagonisms and his encomia require high pitch, tempo, and other such inflections (which linguists refer to as *paralingual* speech), then we ought to expect that he would come off as an intensely colorful personality. In a singularly acoustical environment where a story vanishes as soon as it is uttered, one can't really afford characters that wallow in elusive subtleties of behavior, let alone storytellers who convey those characters in overly restrained or understated ways.

Walter Benjamin drew judicious attention to this when arguing that "genuine storytelling"—by which he was implying stories that are told rather than written and read—was by no means a job "for the voice alone. Rather, in genuine storytelling the hand plays a part which supports what is expressed in a hundred ways with its gestures trained by work."[1] Genuine storytelling is not merely a story, in other words, but a performing art—"a one-person theatre," as the narrator of a short UNESCO documentary on Mongolian oral epic describes.[2] (By the way, you can find that documentary on YouTube, as well as a number of others produced by UNESCO that will allow you to glimpse the diversity and variety of oral-performance styles that exist worldwide, not to mention the skills and creativity inherent in being a traditional bard. A few of note include an Egyptian performance of the Arabic epic of Al-Sirah Al-Hilaliyyah, and a brief history of Tibet's Gesar epic, which is the longest in the world.)

Intriguingly, what late twentieth-century masala films reveal is how, when translated into a visual medium, those paralinguistic characteristics of oral performance can mutate into a character's own kinetic comport, which is to say *his* physical gesturing. In fact, movement, like the utterance—as if an extension *of* the utterance—is crucial and practically compulsory in these films. Don't get me wrong: Movement can certainly take place onscreen absent of any utterance or that utterance's aural extensions (such as music and even sound effects), just as utterances can transpire without wholesale kinetic movement. But rarely, if ever, in these movies does complete stillness come conjoint with complete silence. That is, you almost never get long takes of quiescence *and* quietude together. This, of course, begs the question: Does a culture or community predisposed to orality experience silence, when that silence is in lockstep with stasis, as something akin to what radio culture terms *dead air*? In other words, a mutual lack of kinesis-acoustics might register as an odd and nonsensical *interruption* of a story rather than as a vital component to that story's telling.

Perhaps, then, it will not seem too much of a reach were I to propose that an overly restrained hero in an oral epic might likewise constitute a sort of dead air. Much like those palatial settings, or the slum when vivified as Slum-ness, a warrior-protagonist in oral epic is hardly just a warrior. He is the best warrior—*ever*—much as a hero is not merely swift-footed, but the fastest man—*ever known*. Lovely-haired Helen isn't just lovely; she is the most stunning, best-dressed thing that ever adorned the earth. As for Gilgamesh, he, as we are told at the outset of the first tablet of his story, is

Supreme over other kings, lordly in appearance,
he is the hero, born of Uruk, the goring wild bull.
He walks out in front, the leader,
and walks at the rear, trusted by his companions.
Mighty net, protector of his people,
raging flood-wave who destroys even walls of stone!
Offspring of Lugalbanda, Gilgamesh is strong to
perfection,
son of the august cow, Rimat-Ninsun; ... Gilgamesh is
awesome to perfection.[3]

But Gilgiamesh isn't only perfection. Like so many of the heroes
in these oral epics, Achilles and Helen included, he is also *part
god*. (As for why Gilgamesh and these others would be only *part*
god: That's because otherwise they would be immortal and, so,
where would the dangers lie in their confronting adversaries or
running into clamorous battle?)

Their part–deific status also puts them on a platform that marks
them as entirely beyond us mere mortals, notwithstanding that
they probably did have historical (and mortal) roots. But, now,
unlike you or me, they are super-heroic (and, yes, I'm purposely
associating them with modern-day figures like Superman or
Wonder Woman).[4] Just as critical is that such super-heroism–cum-
partial godliness amplifies their identities in ways that ensure we
never forget them. Who has the more favorable chance of being
venerated and remembered over the long haul: a Beautiful Princess
or an average girl; a Warrior-King who was Born Miraculously
and Performs Marvelous Feats, or a ploughman eking out his
living in a middling grass hut? Bear in mind that whatever values
or moral codes were centrally condensed in these aggrandized
characters would also have far better chance of surviving.

Colorless personalities simply cannot survive mnemonically in
an oral culture,[5] and neither can personalities that lack instantly
understood weight. To endure, they must be what Walter J. Ong
refers to as "heavy" characters[6]—though you may be more familiar
with the other literary term for them: "flat." They, like their deeds,
must be memorably enlarged and fantastically inflated. But you

need not trust me or Ong alone. As Eric Havelock colorfully describes in *The Greek Concept of Justice*,

> In the context of military confrontation they become generals, commanders of great masses of men; in their civil aspect they become kings and queens and princes and princesses, grandiose versions of members of that public for whose benefit the oral epic is being composed.[7]

Apologies to those readers who may still retain the belief that Homer's ceremonial style (or that of the many poets whom we now know solely as "Anonymous") was molded to suit his aristocratic audiences, who were eager to see themselves reflected in an epically lofty and elevated light. To be sure, the connections between bards and the royal elite were often very real, much as Mamadou Kouyate explained vis-a-vis his own relationship to Mali's princes. But as Havelock worthily counsels—perhaps shockingly to some ears—it makes more sense to think of the heroic tradition "as though it were a technical convenience."[8] As much as we may like to search out particularities of character with which we can personally identify, or to conceive of Odysseus, Penelope, or Son-Jara as being human like us, each of those characters was also—and perhaps more indispensably—functioning as a vessel in the service of the organization of knowledge.

Notes

1 Benjamin, "Storyteller," 93.
2 It's titled "Mongol Tuuli: Mongolian Epic," and you can retrieve it from www.youtube.com/watch?v=ZPVyKJinpf4.
3 This passage appears on Tablet I.
4 Some scholars would certainly disagree with me on this. In her *Tales of Literacy for the 21st Century*, written with Stephanie Gottwald, Maryanne Wolf differentiates the superheroes of comic books from the "human heroes like Odysseus and Achilles" because the former "can go beyond all the expectations that circumscribe them with talents that perennially defy normal limitations like human speed" (120). But I think we need to make space for how orally inflected heroes might

also metamorphose through the ages due to permutations in culture and technology, as well as in religious beliefs and practices.

5 Ong, *Orality and Literacy*, 68.
6 Ibid.
7 Havelock, *Greek Concept*, 97.
8 Havelock, *Preface to Plato*, 119.

References

Benjamin, Walter. "The Storyteller." *Theory of the Novel: A Historical Approach*. Ed. Michael McKeown. Baltimore: Johns Hopkins University Press, 2000. 77–93.

The Epic of Gilgamesh. Trans. Maureen Gallery Kovacs. Electronic edition by Wolf Carnahan, 1998. Academy of Ancient Texts. Retrieved August 8, 2017, from www.ancienttexts.org/ library/Mesopotamian/ gilgamesh.

Havelock, Eric A. *The Greek Concept of Justice: From Its Shadow in Homer to Its Substance in Plato*. Cambridge, MA: Harvard University Press, 1978.

———. *Preface to Plato*. Cambridge, MA: Belknap Press of Harvard University Press, 1963.

"Mongol Tuuli: Mongolian Epic." *YouTube*. UNESCO. Published on September 27, 2009. Retrieved July 22, 2019, from www.youtube.com/watch?v=ZPVyKJinpf4.

Ong, Walter J. *Orality and Literacy: The Technologizing of the Word*. London: Methuen, 1982.

Wolf, Maryanne, with Stephanie Gottwald. *Tales of Literacy for the 21st Century*, by Maryanne Wolf. Oxford: Oxford University Press, 2016.

29 Is *anti*psychological necessarily unreal?

When Walter Benjamin set about trying to characterize the great oral stories of yore, he did so by highlighting their refusal to provide the sort of psychological motivations and explanations that most readers of literature today anticipate. But he also shrewdly noted why this was the case: "There is nothing that commends a story to memory more effectively than that chaste compactness which precludes psychological analysis."[1] The Spanish philosopher José Ortega y Gasset was somewhat more scathing in his critique of the deficiency of the psychological in the ancient world—a world that, to him, seemed "a mere body without any inner recesses and secrets."[2] Only during the Renaissance, in his eyes, would discovery arise of "the inner world in all its vast extension, the *me ipsum* [I myself], the consciousness, the subjective."[3]

But even if Ortega is right, the fact that print became the norm during the very period which he esteems warrants our asking the following: Could the private, isolated, and non-collective nature of reading, which print helped exponentially to foster, have had some bearing on the humans *in* storytelling plumbing the inner recesses of their being with ever-increasing intensity—and, so, coming evermore to privilege the individualized agency of the self? As for those ripe emotional exchanges that befit an oral economy, they somewhat necessarily breed an antipsychological aspect to narrative presentation. It's inscription that phylogenetically made space in continuous narrative for breeding the opposite, for the further and further expedition into one's own single, discrete human mind as an existential terrain disconnected from the group. Indeed, literary scholar Erich Kahler[4] observed more than half a century ago how the evolution of the novel reflects this shifting consciousness, with a narrator's observational post becoming progressively more internalized. In other words, the experience of events relocates or is displaced from an outer space into an inner space—not to mention, that this relocation enables both writer and reader to take in wider and wider circles of the external world. (Of course, this prompts yet more potentially discomfiting questions about what the putative realism of a psychologically driven novel like Gustave Flaubert's *Madame Bovary* might really mean!)

By no means should we forget either that the most popular and all-the-rage literary form during the Renaissance was the chivalric romance. So popular was the genre, in fact, that, in the early 1600s, Miguel de Cervantes would hilariously lampoon the extent to which people were obsessed with it in his novel *Don Quixote*. Of greater relevance for us, however, is literary theorist Northrop Frye's admission that, what distinguishes these chivalric romances most essentially from the (presumably more respectable) genre of the novel is their dichotomous conceptions of characterization: "The romancer does not attempt to create 'real people' so much as stylized figures which expand into psychological archetypes."[5] While Frye may will there upon associate the romance hero, heroine, and villain with archetypal aspects of the human psyche—Jung's proposed libido (psychic energy), anima (female in man), and shadow (repressed parts of the individual), respectively—what he says also inadvertently reflects what these characters share with those of folklore: They are agents of action, reducible to what they *do* rather than to what they are internally. Hence Vladimir Propp's ability to sort out the stylized "types" that inhabit Russian folklore: the Villain, the Helper, the Hero, the False Hero, the Princess, her Father, and so forth.[6]

Once again, we see the ways in which ethical qualities— such as virtue, justice, temperance, and the like—are, in the oral circumstance, completely entwined with the situations in which they are exhibited. As David Abram explains, oral utterances were always

> called forth by particular social situations; they had no apparent existence independent of those situations. ... "Justice" and "temperance" were thus experienced as living occurrences, as *events*. Arising in specific situations, they were inseparable from the particular persons or actions that momentarily embodied them.[7]

Perhaps that's why, for the many of us who were inculcated from our earliest days into literate praxes, a character like Gilgamesh appears highly schizophrenic (in the literary sense of that term). As readers schooled in, and habituated to, exhibitions of the intricacies of an inner life, we expect and anticipate that psychological motivations will be provided—or, at the least, that they will be hinted at enough for us to extract or discern them for ourselves. We're far less inclined these days to accept that a character might, in one moment, embody hubris and, immediately in the next, become the active epitome of virtue. Even less predisposed are we to accepting without issue that the character of a king like Gilgamesh is *always* predominantly that of a hero who "has seen everything," who is "[s]upreme over other kings" and the semi-divine "protector of his people." If today we tend instead to muse interpretively over the *incongruities* we observe in his behavior, that's largely because we have the inscriptive means by which to engage with his story. We can poke and prod it like an archaeologist—which is, of course, something that the epic's original participants were considerably less able or in wont of doing.

As a result, we need to be cautious about not *over* reading the contents of a work like *Gilgamesh*. While I'm not suggesting we should refrain from reading the epic "our way," we ought, at least, to acknowledge that we are reading it differently; that our very capacity to "excavate" the text—such as through intimately comparing what Gilgamesh does on "page 43" to what he did

Figure 29.1 Scenes from the Bayeux Embroidery, including men staring at Halley's Comet and Harold at Westminster (Creative Commons/Public Domain). "[P]ictures predate the written word by a large margin," states the comic-book historian Scott McCloud,[8] although there are indeed words—Latin *tituli*—in this embroidered chronicle comprising some 50 scenes of the Norman Conquest of England in 1066. Having been stitched in 1070, only a few years after that conquest, its contents obviously didn't derive from an oral passing down of events through the ages. Nevertheless, the tapestry's sequential storytelling possesses many of the characteristics that align with oral inflection: an emphasis on violent actions; a flat, diagrammatic depiction of events; an amplification (through simplification) of those events, further compounded by the use of bright colors; and a frontality of the figures that renders them iconic or notational,[9] with their gesturing/sign-pointing even serving as an adjunct to speech. (In case you are thinking, "Well, yeah, because it's essentially a comic strip in cloth, so what else would you expect?" stay tuned for the sequel to this book, where you'll find out just how misguided that assumption is!)

on "page 2"—generates an entirely different interpretive context for the epic. We have come to psychologize so much in our contemporary storytelling environment (what was character X's real motivation? why subconsciously did Y do that?). So, it probably behooves us when reading oral epic—or watching those 1970s-1990s masala films where characters similarly wear their characters on their sleeves—to keep in mind oral epic's sensible resistance to expected or obligatory interpretation. Consider this an unintended boon: You don't have to puzzle over unspoken motivations the way some professors might anticipate or even goad you to do!

Notes

1 Benjamin, "Storyteller," 82.
2 Ortega y Gasset, "From *Meditations*," 282.
3 Ibid.
4 Kahler, *Inward Turn*.
5 Frye, *Anatomy of Criticism*, 304. This appears in the fourth of that book's essays, "Rhetorical Criticism: Theory of Genres."
6 See Propp, *Morphology of the Folktale*.
7 Abram, *Spell of the Sensuous*, 110.
8 McCloud, *Understanding Comics*, 141.
9 Art historian Geeta Kapur employs some of these terms to describe the frontality common to the Indian popular arts, although she contends their frontality is modeled after devotional engagement with a religious icon (see Prasad, *Ideology of the Hindi Film*, 18).

References

Abram, David. *The Spell of the Sensuous: Perception and Language in a More-Than-Human World.* New York: Vintage Books, 1997.

Benjamin, Walter. "The Storyteller." *Theory of the Novel: A Historical Approach.* Ed. Michael McKeown. Baltimore: Johns Hopkins University Press, 2000. 77–93.

Frye, Northrop. *Anatomy of Criticism: Four Essays.* Princeton, NJ: Princeton University Press, 1990.

Kahler, Erich. *The Inward Turn of the Narrative*. Evanston, IL: Northwestern University, 1987.

McCloud, Scott. *Understanding Comics: The Invisible Art*. New York: William Morrow Paperbacks, 1994.

Ortega y Gasset, José. "From *Meditations on Quixote.*" *Theory of the Novel: A Historical Approach*. Ed. Michael McKeown. Baltimore: Johns Hopkins University Press, 2000. 271–293.

Prasad, M. Madhava. *Ideology of the Hindi Film: A Historical Construction*. New Delhi: Oxford University Press, 1998.

Propp, V. *The Morphology of the Folktale*. Trans. Laurence Scott. Austin: University of Texas Press, 2009.

30 Animating abstract knowledge

While Gilgamesh was by all accounts a genuine historical figure, as we already addressed, the exigencies of oral transmission through time led to his being sculpted as somebody more than human; as a figure with totemic energy and might. The same applies to the antagonists that he and other epical heroes like him are forced to combat. In the case of Gilgamesh, there's Humbaba, the monstrous, terrorizing giant who reigns over the Cedar Forest. In *Beowulf*, there's Grendel, the monstrous giant who terrorizes the Danes' mead hall. Homeric epic provides us the one-eyed, monstrous, terrorizing Cyclops, whom Odysseus has to outwit. In Mongolian epic, meanwhile, it's a many-headed ogre known as the *manggus* that the heroes must often battle and rout. Or, consider the anthropomorphic trickster figures who inhabit the oral stories of so many cultures—Ashanti, Cree, Chinese, Irish, Jewish, Welsh, Yoruba, and more (some even say the *Odyssey* is a stitched-together composite of trickster tales). And what of the Hindu *Ramayana*'s evil King Ravana, with his ten sprouting heads? Or, in antithesis to Ravana as a "negative character" (in keeping here with masala film-speak), what of the devoted and enterprisingly trickster-like monkey-god Hanuman? We ought also to draw attention to that Bull of Heaven which, at the behest of the goddess Ishtar, is cast down to destroy Gilgamesh's subjects and their crops.

Long ago—in 1914, to be exact—the pioneering anthropologist Franz Boas concluded that the "essential problem" when it came to the nature of mythical thought entailed figuring out why "human tales are preferably attached to animals, celestial bodies, and other personified phenomena of nature."[1] For instance, that Bull of Heaven is said to be an anthropomorphized version of the constellation Taurus. The *manggus* is purported to represent uncontrollable natural forces. And Ravana's multiple heads are ostensibly stand-ins for abstracted forms of (depending on whom you ask) his acute learning, his knowledge of love, or his emotions. While many of these beings' origins are lost to the mists of time, etiological hypothesizing persists. In fact, let's partake of some ourselves: Was the Cyclops originally some sort of local daemon—or how about the inventive consequence of the skulls of prehistoric dwarf elephants, which the ancients found? Or was hyperbolized vitalization of a severe birth defect with which infants could be born? Let's keep going.

Could the fire-breathing dragon of *Beowulf*—whose vengeance erupts because a slave pilfered a cup from his underground treasure hoard—have been representative of fiery lava streams or some treacherous volcanic activity of yore? Or was that beast possibly meant to represent the Devil? What if maybe it was, or became over time, an amalgamation of both? What if it began as natural force that then, with the arrival of Christianity, got transmuted into Hellfire? (Some have even argued that the *Epic of Gilgamesh* is, at heart, a strikingly nonabstract "textbook" delineating natural forces of another kind—the ancient Sumerian astronomical world.) What if the wolf totem in Mongolian mythology was a way of pictorially depicting the Mongols' Turkish vassals as inferior as a species? Could the same apply to Hanuman even? That is, not only might he represent some past individual or, just as viably, the conflation of an entire people into a single character, but that in his doing so as an *animal* avatar ensured that he would forever remain subordinate to the human avatar, Rama, whom he served? And to return to *Gilgamesh*: What if Humbaba were a singular enemy stand-in for the Neanderthals? Indeed, could the same apply to the *Odyssey*'s cave-dwelling, cannibalistic Cyclops? Or, to turn the lens no less questioningly on the one posing these questions: Is this my own historically and scientifically motivated way of animating these epics, of making them more "present" and "authentic" to me?

No matter the answer to these lines of inquiry, there's one thing we can guarantee about such transmogrified creatures: Whether as people transformed into trolls and giants, or astrological formations transmuted into fiery, snorting, and pilitlessly enraged beasts, they have far more totemic power than do earthly mortal figures. And they certainly have more than nonhuman and altogether abstract forces that otherwise come without faces, without bodies, without emotion or intent. According to David Abram, the "more-than-human-terrain" that pervades the storytelling of deeply oral cultures—by which he means one alive with inclusive of animals, trees, clouds, planets—places both the poet and his listeners "within a huge story that is visibly unfolding around us ...."[2] No wonder that so many children's stories today—like so many fables, folk tales, and fairy tales—pivot on animal characters: adventurous mice, lost birds, lame ducks, fantastic foxes.

On a related note, I vividly recall my first time teaching an introductory literature course, primarily because its opening weeks coincided with 9/11, the day when the World Trade Center's twin towers were brought down by Al-Qaeda operatives in commercial planes. Only days after, the literary term *personification* arose in class, and the visual example that leapt immediately to my mind was one I had only just seen in the *New York Times*. New York City children had been asked, as a form of trauma therapy, to draw their experiences of 9/11. One particular illustrator had given two appropriately lean and towering buildings human faces: downturned mouths and dejectedly closed eyes from which tears were trickling. Upon my drawing this depiction on the whiteboard, immediately the my students understood—no, viscerally felt—the compact power inherent in those previously inanimate buildings. The towers had suddenly become living creatures and, so, entities that now could also *act*. They could weep in the knowledge of their obliterated futures or (were they to be wrested from their inorganic positioning on the whiteboard and orally animated as giants) become twin Goliaths soon to be felled.

And when in the form of antagonists, how much more powerful these creatures are, whether as vehicles of evil or danger, or of unbridled power, or even—when at the hand of a spiteful, immortal god—life's fickleness. As Walter J. Ong reminds us, in the absence of

> elaborate analytic categories that depend on writing to structure knowledge at a distance from lived experience, oral cultures must conceptualize knowledge with more or less close reference to the human lifeworld, assimilating the alien, objective world to the more immediate, familiar interaction of human beings.[3]

In other words, abstractions as well as inanimate objects and events (drought, ethical tenets, theological concerns with death, urban skyscrapers, the tenuous boundaries between nature and culture) are, through personification or organic embodiment, treated as dynamic aspects of the human lifeworld. They are, in a sense, absorbed and made interactive with the domain of human activity.

Again, which of the following pairings do you think would qualify as more memorable—and even more indispensably perhaps, as *worthier* of remembering: a hero fighting a "real" or "authentic" sort of human (someone who resembles and acts like you and me, or our neighbors, or the average Jo/e you pass in an airport); *or* a beast that embodies something otherworldly, potentially supernatural and, in that capacity, dangerously unknown? We're talking about a creature so fierce that it threatens the very survival and perpetuation of Your People. What possibly could more vividly manifest a world of "Us against Them" than when those "Them" are animals, monsters, or beasts living in caves? (By the way, these are all phrases that American politicians have used to describe their nation's proclaimed nemeses.) No wonder, too, that the Us—which is to say, the hero or heroes battling on behalf of their People—must be pretty terrifi c: royal, semi-divine, wily, and/or exceptionally brave.

True, sometimes the hero-beast rivalry is more Cain and Abel-like, in that the heightened horror comes in warfare between family relations, blood brothers even, who are vying for rule. Still, it's the intensely, if flatly, colorful and concrete qualities of the battle that follows—that *must* follow, we might say—that are of consequence here, as they are the very ones that accommodate the story's survival in the oral ecology. In fact, the oral requirement that a narrative be memorable ultimately steers that narrative *away* from verisimilitude, from any appearance of being true, real, or believable, and toward a texture much more familiar to and aligned with myth.

Notes

1 Boas, "Mythology and Folk-Tales," 410.
2 Abram, *Spell of the Sensuous*, 163.
3 Ong, *Orality and Literacy*, 42.

References

Abram, David. *The Spell of the Sensuous: Perception and Language in a More-Than-Human World.* New York: Vintage Books, 1997.
Boas, Franz. "Mythology and Folk-Tales of the North American Indians." *The Journal of American Folklore* 27, 106 (1914): 374–410.
Ong, Walter J. *Orality and Literacy: The Technologizing of the Word.* London: Methuen, 1982.

31 The absence of irony, the pleasure of parody

Some years ago, I was presenting the bones of this book's content in a faculty colloquium at the college where I teach. When I was done and the time came for questions, one of my colleagues from my very own English department raised his hand. Was it really possible, he asked, with something close to incredulity (if not outright disbelief), that the films I was talking about exhibited virtually *no* signs of irony? To him, as an individual who had devoted his professional career to literature, particularly to American modernists like Ernest Hemingway and William Faulkner, a lack of irony seemed inconceivable.

I held my ground though. After all, I had screened dozens upon dozens of Bollywood's twentieth-century box-office hits, and irony had indeed been almost completely nonapparent. Most definitely, irony resided in the *art* cinema of India—which is to say, that body of work that, at the time, was referred to as *parallel* cinema because of its serving as a counterpart or alternative to Bombay commercial cinema. But when it came to the popular movies hugely popular with mass audiences, irony was almost entirely absent. Dramatic irony was sometimes present, as was also parody (ubiquitously, in fact); but free-floating irony—only very, very, very rarely. Just to be safe, let's go over how I'm distinguishing these various literary terms, since they are sometimes inappropriately used as synonyms for each other.

Let's start with parody, which entails a lampooning of some preexisting—and, thereby, preknown—event, activity, or entertainment. Think of when *Saturday Night Live* put Melissa McCarthy behind a podium in the guise of White House Press Secretary "Sean Spicey" or when a film like *Shaun of the Dead* comically mocks a decades-long spate of zombie movies (much as *Spaceballs* sends up *Star Wars*, and *Airplane!*, the airplane disaster films of the 1970s). Ever seen those memes of famous Renaissance portraiture where the faces have been digitally replaced to reflect alternative ethnicities, genders, or cultural contexts? Or how about the expressionistically aghast screamer in Edvard Munch's *The Scream* supplanted by the Pillsbury doughboy? Even when Don Quixote goes on his 800-page expedition as an errant knight, he's being sent by Cervantes in imitation of the hundreds of romances *both* men have read; so, it's anticipated that we have some familiarity with the chivalric romance if we're going to catch the humor in Cervantes' send-up of the genre. In fact, because people cannot possibly parody—or catch the parody in—what is *un*familiar, often readers who have lost contact with what's being burlesqued will find the material baffling, banal, even silly or senseless (yes, even apropos a classic like *Don Quixote*). At other times, they may unintentionally or purposely read it (again, Don Quixote included) against its intended grain.

The etymology of the word parody, in fact, explicitly signals this knowledge of a text that is precursory but also contemporary—which is to say, still living, still resonant—given its derivation from the ancient Greek *par-*, beside, and *ode*, a song. Indeed, in the Bollywood context, often the pleasure of parody comes by way of song, whether as renowned lyrics humorously reworked, or legendary tunes and even orality-friendly jingles that are gratifyingly sent off course. Even more, memorable characters from prior movies can make an appearance, as can lines of dialogue, props, costumes, settings, or even wholesale reworkings of sketches or songs. (Of course, reprises like this are also suggestive of the oral inclination to repeat the past—not out of laziness or lack of imagination, but because doing so is the only way to keep what is still culturally resonant *alive*.)

Dramatic irony operates in similar fashion, whereby the addressees must possess some knowledge in advance in order for them to glean a second level of meaning in the text. Unlike parody, though, this dramatic or literary device isn't contingent on spoofing. In fact, let's turn by way of example to one of the most distinguished examples of dramatic irony in action, which you can find in a tragedy, Sophocles' *Oedipus Rex*. See, when theatergoers gathered in ancient Athens to witness that play, they did so already knowing what King Oedipus himself doesn't know at its outset—namely, that, long ago, he killed his own father, the former Theban king, and married his own mother, with whom he now has several children. In other words, *he's* the one responsible for the disease now blighting the Theban kingdom. So, imagine him strutting the stage, raging at the individual responsible for his subjects' suffering, spouting promises that said individual will pay. And when he declares in vociferous tones that he, Oedipus, will bring the truth to light (in spite of the blind seer Tiresius imploring him not to), and that he, Oedipus, will banish the culprit—*that's* dramatic irony. And only because those Athenian spectators preknow what Oedipus initially doesn't that they are able to catch all the ironic implications of his pledges and threats.

Now, imagine taking away such a vital piece of information from an audience or reader. Do so and—well, at least figuratively speaking—you are left with irony alone. The "alone" here is key. You, the addressee, have to figure out on your own—let's say while reading a short story—that what is semantically intended may actually be the opposite of what the narrator or character says. Perhaps the best, most concise example is when, at the end of Kate Chopin's short story "The Story of an Hour, the protagonist Mrs. Mallard dies, and we are informed in the final sentence that "When the doctors came they said she had died of heart disease—of the joy that kills."[1] This joy, those doctors surmised, was due to her husband—whom only an hour before she was told was dead—suddenly and (obviously) unexpectedly showing up at the door. But in order for you, as the reader, to discern that the return of her husband is not what really killed Mrs. Mallard, and that you should not take the doctors' prognostication literally (including their postmortem diagnosis of her ecstasy at his return), you have to connect the dots yourself. You have to recall how, at the story's outset, Chopin reveals that Mrs. Mallard has a weak heart. You have to remember how, not long after receiving word of her husband's death, Mrs. Mallard's initial grief mutates into a swelling, if bittersweet recognition of her emancipation; of her suddenly, as a female, having become free. This you need to do because Chopin never explicitly states that this is the sudden reversal of fortune that leads to Mrs. Mallard's demise. Chopin never tells us outright that what kills her protagonist is not the joyous shock of her husband's return, but the shocking recognition that her anticipated liberty has been crushed. So, if we are not able to make the leap that Chopin anticipates, if we cannot in our own mind close that semantic gap through filling in the blanks, then, alas, we will read that last line literally instead of ironically and, thus, completely miss what Chopin intends for us to take away from her story.

I have indeed had students who were not prepared for—by which I mean, they had not yet been suitably literately inculcated into thinking that—an author might mean something other than what she was saying. And I can't really blame them. With parody, there are no missing puzzle pieces (provided, of course, that you know the original text being caricatured). Irony, on the other hand, prizes the missing puzzle piece. It demands that you, as the reader, engage in some mental detective work—which is, at heart, just that: a kind of *work*. You must figure out not only what this indefinite signifier in "The Story of an Hour" means— but that it's an indefinite signifier; and because most likely you are reading Chopin's short story privately and silently to yourself, you must to do this work entirely on your own. Worse yet, the only way to construe irony's meaning appropriately requires knowing—requires a veritable training in the foreknowledge— that your search is for something that is *not there*.

Now, think about irony in the context of an oral community. Can there be anything lonelier than the disengagement from the group that irony mandates? Even more importantly, can there be any literary device or technique more in danger of threatening a story's communication through time? Remember that, in many instances, what is being transmitted is a people's history, their culture and traditions. Who, in that circumstance, would favor the kind of uncertain, ambiguous, indefinite, fill-in-the-blank relationship that irony compels? Traditional stories cannot afford the distance that irony wedges between a story's teller and that teller's audience. Rather, the audience for those stories depends at every point on the teller's judgments about characters and events. Or, as Robert Scholes and Robert Kellogg more force-fully put it, audiences of traditional stories willingly adopt "the narrator's god-like view."[2] And that god-like view, which is born of necessity, not ego or personal authoritarianism, precludes so many of the characteristics that today we are told are sug-gestive of sophisticated literature: subtext (underlying meaning that is not explicitly stated); subjectivity (capturing what exists in someone's mind or consciousness, taking on their idiosyncratic perspective); and, of course, irony. By the way, a diachronic or "distant reading" of the contents of any anthology of Western literature would certify not only Walter J. Ong's contention that "the longer the writing (and print) tradition endures, the heavier the ironic growth becomes,"[3] but that the same applies to subtext and subjectivity. These are decidedly literary techniques, in other words, in the sense that they are extensively tied to what *litera*, the alphabetic letter, permits.

So, what does that say about the inherent instability of language—a theme that philosophers in more recent decades have earnestly tendered? In a very cursory (and, ergo, somewhat unjust) summary of their claims, these intellectuals emphasize language's endless ambiguity, its variability and altogether prob-lematical nature. That may sound persuasive to those of us who intensively scrutinize an author's moves on the page, and who do so for the purposes of teasing out the texts inconsistencies and inner contradictions. But would an oral culture be desirous of reveling in that sort of contrived and deconstructive play with meaning? Would they even be predisposed toward engaging in such an impractical game?

That's not to say orally inflected narratives don't take great delight in fashioning and flaunting language's slipperiness,

JOHN
GARDNER
Grendel

"An extraordinary achievement."
—*The New York Times*

Figure 31.1 Cover of John Gardner's 1971 novel *Grendel*. Courtesy of Penguin Random House LLC. If you've read this far in *Before Literature*, you're sure to find Gardner's novel

whether by way of puns, bawdy double-entendres, or jokes that arise due to the misheard or misinterpreted. But the success of these is contingent on that slipperiness being recognized. This is a slipperiness of language of which participants are intended to be fully *aware*. What some of those modern philosophers highlight, contrastingly, are authorial slips, deferrals, and instabilities in meaning that are built into language itself. Moreover, the inconsistencies of language that they study, theorize, prove, and even put into practice are generally sight-dominant—which is to say, pretty much exclusive to inscription, to written text alone. This doubly amplifies my earlier enquiry as to whether their delighting in the instability and precariousness-apart of language would be efficacious, let alone even possible, in an oral ecology. In short, those modern philosophers' study of language rests on a "stage of consciousness" (to borrow from Hayden White[4]) that only the convenience of writing permits. Their work might even represent the current alphabetically literate limit or frontier of our age's irony-infused intellectualism. Of course, this is something positive, not negative—much in the same way that literacy

Caption for Figure 31.1 (Continued)

remarkable for its radical departure from an oral way of knowing—and so, too, from *Beowulf*, from which Gardner plucked his central character. The story—Grendel's story, from Grendel's point of view—is told in the first person, often as stream of consciousness. As the story's protagonist, Grendel is startlingly individualistic, acutely self-conscious, and obsessed with the philosophical nature and agency of human language. In other words, this is a monster wrested from the original oral epic and refashioned for a text-based audience, one that has not only gone private, but that revels in gray uncertainty; feels little necessity to shore up or conserve the collective point of view; and has the capacity, and perhaps even self-aware obligation now, to see the Other's point of view. A story without resolution and one shot through with irony, *Grendel* is as removed as one can conceivably get from a story that had to be composed and imparted by exclusively oral means.

and, even more, textualism, or the analysis of texts, are what have allowed us conceptually to identify orality at all!⁵

If print storytellers can range where oral storytellers cannot, that's largely because the latter are not authors in the way we moderns conceive that term. So, perhaps, I should call them by the name often contemporarily allotted them: "Anonymous." Unlike the modern author, Anonymous is one in a long line of rhetorical weavers, stitching together traditional stories into the larger fabric of an epic, so as to perpetuate the memory (through his own prodigious memory) of his people's history and cultural sense of self. For this reason, Anonymous generally refrains from advancing any techniques that would make the history of his people too personally his. This is hardly to deny Anonymous his artistry. It's simply that artistry is differently directed, differently driven. In fact, the enormity of any Anonymous' vocation no doubt produced a qualitative spectrum of poets—from mediocre to virtuosic—just as today's novelists can reflect a range of capabilities, in terms of style, tone, versatility, and substance.

We can see the span of this artistry reflected even in the block-buster movies of twentieth-century Bollywood. For, while the industry during the 1970s–1990s was often critically disparaged for churning out formula films that lacked all originality, during the Golden Age of Indian cinema (1950s–1960s), directors could earn major plaudits for their superior direction. One of these bene-ficiaries was Mehboob Khan, the director of *Mother India* (1957). Film reviewers deemed his epic drama superior for its plotline, high production values, and use of natural settings—not suspecting that *Mother India* also subscribed almost completely to the oral episteme of narrative. In tandem with its episodic structure, complete with flashbacks, after all, were spirited, agonistic dialogues that steered the film toward melodrama and an anti-psychological bent; a visual spectacularity that was outwardly oriented and unambiguous in meaning; and ample allusions to the mythologically preknown.

Intriguingly, director Mehboob Khan grew up never having learned to read or write, which may well have aided him in crafting a film that could reach across his nation's audiences, not only aesthetically but also epistemically. The film's oral underpinnings may also account for why *Mother India*, in spite of its ardent and even jingoistic nationalism—which, by the way, is never presented in ironic terms—proved just as resonant for Hausa villagers in Nigeria, as well as for spectators in Egypt, China, Spain, Greece, the former Soviet Union, and Ghana. Ultimately, *Mother India*'s Indian patriotism *transcended* India, precisely because that patriotism could be experienced as a more general, universal, oral embrace of collective unity and of the desired restoration of traditional order. In other words, the film could be processed no less as *Mother Egypt* or *Mother Ghana*.

Don't get the renewed impression, though, that the construction and performance of oral narrative precludes variety and skill. The *Iliad* and *Odyssey* alone show how different oral epics can be in tone, atmosphere, intentions, and focus. So different are these two epics, in fact—one a comparatively taut, localized tragedy about war; the other a sprawling, comically oriented adventure story—that some scholars insist they could not possibly have been composed by the same poet. Whatever your own belief about their "authorial origins," the *Iliad* and *Odyssey* speak to the variability and diversity that existed in heroic epic, notwithstanding the pressures that orality placed on the form. The same might be said of those superhit Bollywood formula films of yore, which extend from graphically violent to more family-friendly, while also varying in terms of genre. They might be comedies, social melodramas, crime dramas, or "curry westerns"—all while remaining firmly rooted in oral inflection.

Notes

1 "The Story of an Hour," which you can find easily online, was first published in the December 6, 1894, issue of *Vogue*.

2 Scholes and Kellogg, *Nature of Narrative*, 50.

3 Ong, *Orality and Literacy*, 103.

4 Quoted in Higgins, *New Novel, New Wave*, 22.

5 For more on this, see Ong's section in *Orality and Literacy* on "Textualists and Deconstructionists," 162–165.

References

Chopin, Kate. "The Story of an Hour." *Kate Chopin: Complete Novels & Stories*. New York: Library of America, 2000: 756–758. Retrieved August 19, 2017, from http://storyoftheweek.loa.org/2014/01/the-story-of-hour.html.

Higgins, Lynn A. *New Novel, New Wave, New Politics: Fiction and Representation of History in Postwar France*. Lincoln: University of Nebraska Press, 1996.

Ong, Walter J. *Orality and Literacy: The Technologizing of the Word*. London: Methuen, 1982.

Scholes, Robert, and Robert Kellogg. *The Nature of Narrative*. Oxford: Oxford University Press, 1968.

32 Is there an oral chronosense?

Chronosense may sound like a fancy, if nonsensical word, but its meaning is pretty straightforward. Deriving from the world of neuroscience, chronosense signifies our human sense experience of time. (*Chrono-* comes from the Greek for "time"—familiar to you, no doubt, in such words as *chronology* and *chronicle*.) Our perception of time is a neuropsychological process, in other words, and so, rather than being time-bound (ironically enough), time is entirely subject to variability. Attend a riveting movie and time passes briskly. Attend a boring lecture, by contrast, and time lags and drags, slow and sluggish as a clichéd snail. We shape time in our own image, we might say.

But if our sense of time's duration and the events that unfold within it are not natural, wouldn't that mean that oral communities might experience time differently? Or, put another way, if human perceptions are influenced by the processes through which we select, organize, and interpret stimuli—processes that are often culturally learned—should we thereby infer that the personal experience and communal understanding of time might vary radically between oral societies and those structured on the basis of literacy (with their 24-hour cycle, timers, clocks, firm dates, and the like)?

I vividly recall my unlettered grandmother in her elderly years sitting on the veranda of her suburban New Delhi bungalow, marking when it was time for afternoon tea, and then, later, for the cooking of the evening meal. This she did by watching the shadow that slowly, but dependably—"like clockwork," as literates would paradoxically say—creep up the veranda wall. Time, for her, was an experience far more connected with her natural environment: daylight, moonlight, seasons, stars, the arid heat, the monsoon rains. If that sounds alluring, it's only because we've lost many of these connections and, so, read them with a kind of wistful nostalgia. Bear in mind, though, how few of us would be swayed to give up our smartphones and alarm clocks, our weekly calendars that chop up our day into hours, and our chronologies that slice up history century by century, year by year, sometimes even minute by minute. Indeed, few of us, I imagine (if we are to be honest), would willingly give up our experience and possession of a historical past—which many of us consider somehow fuller, richer, more authentic, and truer than any past that mandates its having to be telescoped with the here and now. The latter is, of course, something that orality compels. German philosopher Oswald Spengler even contended that writing had liberated man's consciousness from the "tyranny of the present."[1] Perhaps we ought therefore to revisit the how and why of that oral compulsion before pressing on to the philosophical ramifications of this chronosense.

For societies founded on oral tradition, as Carlo Ginzburg writes, "the memory of the community involuntarily tends to mask and reabsorb changes."[2] So, while cultures whose foundations are lodged in writing tend to think of the past in historical terms—as a terrain itemized and peppered with bits of information and facts, as Walter J. Ong describes—for oral cultures the past is instead "a resonant source for renewing awareness of present existence, which itself is not an itemized terrain either."[3] In other words, the slowly accreted changes through time cannot be assigned, say, to the nineties or the Victorian era. They must instead be ahistorically absorbed, with the orally transmitted epic reflecting the world both *as it has always been* and also *as it is right now*. (Recall the Tiv of Nigeria whom earlier I mentioned as adjusting their past genealogical records—this was in the 1970s—in order to regulate the changed social relations of their contemporary milieu.) But there is well-founded reason for this temporal absorption, as Ginzburg proposes. How else except through tele-scoping the past with the present can that past possibly be carried *into* the present? To be sure, as we have seen, critical changes in social dynamics may bend and twist their way into the fabric of a poem. But even when absorbed, these must yield to what the past ultimately is for oral societies: the domain of one's ancestors—which, of course, includes the domain of one's gods.

So, if the physical and ethical battles that play out in the con-cluding sequences of the masala films that I've cited throughout this book do so in jungles and forests, in the deserts of Rajasthan, or in view of the flames of a wedding's sacred fire (settings I've also previously cited), that's because they also represent a connection to a different sort of real—or to the Real, we might say. For, this Real—with the capitalized R signifying this real as Eternal, not as specific or itemized—is an *ontological* locale: a place that's really about the nature of human being. And what more particularly is being verified through the spectator's experience of this Eternal Real is that all "these things 'were before' also with our ancestors, and became what they are now because of our ancestors." (By the way, that latter quote comes from Eric Havelock, who was talking not about Bombay cinema, but about Homeric epic!)

Might we propose, then, that Time in the oral narrative milieu is experienced more as a cosmographical memory? Or, as David Abram more poetically proposes, language, when enacted as story among oral peoples, functions

> not simply to dialogue with other humans but also to con-verse with the more-than-human cosmos, to renew reci-procity with the surrounding powers of earth and sky, to invoke kinship even with those entities, which, to the civilized mind, are utterly insentient and inert.[4]

For those heavily ensconced in print culture, by contrast, Time becomes History—no, *h*istory, we need say—henceforward converted to a linear accumulation of causes and effects; and to an accumulation experienced not as an integral part of oneself, but as separate and detached from one's own being.

What I'm trying to get at here is that, in the latter circumstance, the tradition of the past as the Past—which is to say, as *sacred*—gets potentially lost. Our ancestral heroes no longer speak through us. Don't misunderstand me: I'm not suggesting literately engaged societies feel any less deeply or intensely when it comes to storytelling, merely that sensations of the numinous or the holy get unavoidably channeled along different avenues. Once storytelling detaches from the oral episteme, burrowing its way deeper and deeper into the written word, how not for us to change ontologically in ways that would impact our, well, *religios*ense? (In *After Literature*, the companion book to this one, I'll address precisely where and how that rechanneling of the sacred occurs.)

This necessarily brings to mind those Kantian notions of art, which earlier we discussed. Can Kant's particular conceptualization of aesthetic experience even exist in milieus where paintings, carvings, woven baskets, musical instruments, and the like serve primarily as extensions of cultural and natural environments[5]? Recall, too, that in the context of oral societies, stories exist primarily as *performance* and, so, can rarely be divorced from their environments—until, of course, someone comes along to transcribe them, typeset them, and, later, digitize various translations of them for a global reading community. Thus is a form originally acoustic and ephemeral transmuted into one that is comparatively fixed, enduring, and visually activated. That past as it comes epically down to us now is experienced foremost through ink on a page or digitally encoded words on a screen. Moreover, it comes with footnotes obligingly providing us background information, cultural and historical context, and explanations about this or that god—all because these are people who are *not* our ancestors. How could that not alter one's chronosense?

Notes

1 Quoted in Goody and Watt, "Consequences of Literacy," 53.
2 Ginzburg, *Cheese and the Worms*, 77.
3 Ong, *Orality and Literacy*, 96.

4 Abram, *Spell of the Sensuous*, 71.
5 This I borrow from Bahn, *Cambridge Illustrated History.*

References

Abram, David. *The Spell of the Sensuous: Perception and Language in a More-Than-Human World.* New York: Vintage Books, 1997.

Bahn, Paul G. *The Cambridge Illustrated History of Prehistoric Art.* Cambridge: Cambridge University Press, 1998.

Ginzburg, Carlo. *The Cheese and the Worms: The Cosmos of a Sixteenth-Century Miller.* Trans. John and Anne Tedeschi. Baltimore: Johns Hopkins University Press, 1980.

Goody, Jack, and Ian Watt, "The Consequences of Literacy," *Literacy in Traditional Societies.* Ed. Jack Goody. Cambridge: Cambridge University Press, 1968. 27–68.

Ong, Walter J. *Orality and Literacy: The Technologizing of the Word.* London: Methuen, 1982.

33 Do intellectuals suffer from alphabetically literate elitism?

Some time ago (in the historical sense), Lawrence Levine argued that the discipline of history generally safeguarded culture in line with how historians had already elected to exhume, define, and interpret it. To make his case—this was in his book *Highbrow/Lowbrow*—he provided an illustrative example from the study of Shakespeare. Levine drew attention to one historian in particular, who, while happily conceding to the Bard's tremendous popularity in nineteenth-century America, attached to that acclamation a painfully propositional *but*: "but," so this author said, Shakespeare's plays in that historical circumstance had been "either produced as vehicles for a popular star … or treated as blood-and-thunder spectacles …." And so Levine wondered: "What was the purpose of this curious '*but*'? Did it really negate, or qualify, or explain the fact of Shakespeare's popularity in any meaningful way? The more I stumbled into these inescapable qualifiers," Levine continues, "the more I concluded that their effective—though not necessarily deliberate—function was to protect the historian and the historian's culture."[1]

Levine ultimately asserted—rightly, I think—that these sorts of value-laden circumventions by historians limit rather than further the dimensions of our capacities to understand culture. Even more, in censoring or marking off some segments of the cultural landscape as warranting exclusion—such as star power and blood-and-thunder spectacle—those historians also deny the actual complexity inherent in any given culture. And here, of course, we need to insert ourselves into Levine's argument, given that those attributes vetoed by Levine's sample historian are entirely in keeping with oral performance. Said historian, we might suggest, was blinded by his own literately inflected positioning and, so, sought, however unconsciously, to get out—and, even more, to get Shakespeare out—from under the oral trappings that he apparently found degrading, belittling, infantilizing and, hence, in danger of eroding a (respectful? upright? epistemically biased?) approach to the Bard's oeuvre. *But*—what orality tells us is that history, certainly as conceived, understood, and fashioned in the Western tradition, is *not* the only domain of truth. It is merely a domain; and as one fundamentally shaped by alphabetic literacy, its truthiness, shall we say, includes not only the wresting of history from the domain of storytelling, but sometimes even of storytelling from itself—such *from itself*, such as when it invests in popular stars and blood-and-thunder spectacle.

By no means am I suggesting that the terms "popular" and "oral" are necessary equivalents. Certainly, few students today conceive of Shakespeare's oeuvre as popular literature, even though that's precisely what his plays were in Elizabethan times. Now, the Bard's language is too archaic and sophisticated for the ordinary individual to follow. Further—and in significant keeping with Levine's original argument—the plays' more elevated aspects tend to get foregrounded, while their earthier elements, both in language and performance (their more universal appeals, ironically enough) are forced into retirement or, at least, into the shadows. We might say that, by reason of both distance and decorum, Shakespeare's particular symbiosis of the oral and the literate has undergone a *literization* over time. One apprehension then becomes that, not unlike the historian protecting the historian's culture, the protection becomes of a poetic culture bound up with an educated elite.

The same might be said of Homeric epic. Typically, those ancient Greek poems are seriously read, deeply read, and perhaps almost exclusively read in college classrooms. In this way, an originally oral form that was popular—in the sense of its appeal and suitability for a general public—is no longer treated or approached as such. What was once necessarily and acoustically accessible because of its episodic structure, formulary expression, exterior-oriented worldview, and so forth has since mutated, due to distance and cultural unfamiliarity, into a form of *cultural capital*. By this I mean—or, rather, am borrowing from sociologist Pierre Bourdieu[2]—that Homer has been reduced (or elevated, depending on your point of view) to a kind of symbolic currency for those cadres of people who can afford an advanced education, including perhaps learning to read Homer in Greek. Thus has a form that shares something substantial with masala films and many a Hollywood blockbuster been the original a way of demonstrating your status as cultured or refined. (If my putting Bollywood and Homer into the same sentence still sends shivers down your spine, then you've probably been making good use of that cultural capital!)

To some extent, Homer's passage into becoming a marker of learnedness was unavoidable. When Homeric poetry entered the written and then printed canon, it had little recourse but to shift from what once it had been—namely, the "culmination" of an oral narrative art, as Robert Scholes and Robert Kellogg declare—to the initiating agent of of written literature.[3] And that passage would now result in Homeric poetry being, and needing to be, historicized. Indeed, what Scholes and Kellogg's word "culmination" acknowledges is that the art of the oral form was now destined to deteriorate in the classical context, given that storytelling would gradually relocate to a form increasingly imagined and conceived for the page. And, of course, that is just how historians do history: for the page.

So, let's return to today's commercial culture, to our contemporary arena where narratives are often assigned the label "popular." If that term often tacitly implies that a narrative is comparatively intelligible, that it doesn't mandate a reader or spectator having to mine for subtext or irony—well, that may be in part the byproduct of that narrative operating according to more oral principles. In fact, because the mass-culture industry is so often motivated by profit, we might anticipate that it would be the realm most likely to give audiences "what they want"—which,

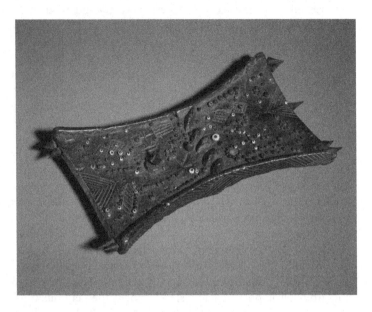

Figure 33.1 The original memory board. Photo of a lukasa ("long
        hand") memory device of the Luba, Democratic Republic
        of Congo. Late 19th or early 20th century. Courtesy
        of Brooklyn Museum. Such boards were used by the
        initiated—the "men of memory"—as mnemonic devices
        for the oral telling of the history of the Luba people. The
        configuration of its beads and carvings were read with
        the right forefinger, prompting the teller's memory of the
        various myths surrounding the origins of the Luba Empire,
        stories of ancestors and ancestresses, and lists of the names of
        royal personages. Note the device's long, curvilinear edges,
        which accommodate its being held in the left hand.[4]

in some cases, might also entail what they epistemically *need*. For,
while more than 50 years of major international initiatives have
worked to reduce illiteracy and provide basic schooling, twenty-
first-century data indicate that "more than 860 million adults
lack minimal capacities to read, write, and calculate."[5] Just think
about that: *860 million*—more than Canada, the UK, and the

USA combined. And two-thirds of those are women, as education specialist Gerald Graff observes, with regions like sub-Saharan Africa hit especially hard (more than 50 percent of its population remains illiterate).[6]

By no means am I suggesting that with literacy comes immediate economic advancement. So many other variables are involved, including social, political and technological transformations that can elevate, but also undercut or undervalue the acquisition of literacy. These can include everything from what neighborhood you live in, to your gender, your geographical mobility, and even who controls the skills of literacy. (In the case of ancient India, it was the caste of priests, the Brahmins, who had that control, and they pretty much maintained their position apropos the sacred scriptures by not sharing those skills with anyone else.) Still—and let us be frank: *Art*, as modernly conceived, is rarely made or envisioned explicitly for the subordinate classes—and, here, I mean subordinate classes no less in industrialized nations than in developing ones. The accrued skills of literacy for those less well off, irrespective of location, may be more functional than advanced or mature enough to permit a trafficking in subtext, symbolism, irony, and the like—those very attributes often extolled of art when in its high literary forms..

But it's also not merely a case of *need*. Just as possible is that the reticulate attributes that comprise the oral episteme can be more comfortably—and even more naturally—assimilated. Keep in mind those children's books and fairy tales, which earlier we discussed, not to mention the Star Wars franchise and the current spate of superhero movies. And while we're on the topic of popular film: Take a look at the characteristics that film historian David Bordwell teased out of 1970s–1990s Hong Kong cinema. This he did to emphasize for his Western readers that popular genre's "distinct aesthetic."[7] Only look at how strikingly familiar these norms actually are (the words in quotation marks are his explicitly):

Non-contemplative
Non-realist
"Manichean"'

Loosely plotted (and "kaleidoscopic")
Kinesthetically arousing
Use of flashbacks
Refining tradition (rather than seeking originality)
In favor of formulas and clichés
Brutally violent
Plagiaristic
Tending to "swerve into a happy ending"[8]

What's intriguing about Bordwell's list is, of course, the commonality it shares with the network of norms that we've covered in this book. But equally important to appreciate is the way the oral episteme does not preclude differences and variation when it comes to storytelling. No one, for example, would mistake a a curry western for a chop-suey western (to use the old, self-assigned descriptors), just as no one would mistake *Gilgamesh* for Norse saga. Narratives that share oral underpinnings are fully capable of maintaining their own cultural, linguistic, and textural uniqueness—much the same way that "Machiavellian" novels can, notwithstanding that their are always inscribing onto a page.

Yes, Bordwell may have willingly referred to the mainstream Hong Kong film as distinct in its "aesthetic"; but was he employing that term in the same way he might describe a film by Swedish existentialist filmmaker Ingmar Bergman or that Japanese master of the domestic drama, Yasujiro Ozu? The subtitle of his book refers to an "Art of Entertainment," after all. In other words, sometimes the word "art" rhetorically designates a skill or style rather than a judgment on the "beautiful" aspects of a work's construction. Which brings us handily back to Lawrence Levine. In his study of shared public culture in nineteenth-century America, Levine made the following intellectual entreaty to his readers: They—we—should no longer obscure the real nature of that culture by insisting on interpreting the category of the popular aesthetically rather than literally.[9] Why? Because too often, in our judging the popular on the basis of aesthetic criteria, we are already biasing our judgment *against* it.

Awareness of the oral characteristics of narrative, as well as of oral noetics (from the Greek *noesis* for "intelligence" or "thought"), certainly allows for some flexibility regarding these judgmental barriers. I'm hoping, in fact, that we've covered heretofore has already persuaded you that aesthetics—Kantian aesthetics, at least—cannot (and certainly cannot *fairly*) be applied to oral narrative when that narrative is part and parcel of an oral community. To be sure, even the most inscription-oriented individuals can find immense pleasure as well as human connection in reading an Icelandic tale like the *Saga of the Volsungs* (it influenced Richard Wagner's *Ring of the Nibelung*, after all). But what those individuals are reading for and also how they're reading, can never correspond to what that narrative represented to the prelit poet singing of its dragon-slaying hero to his prelit community.

And yet, there are even *novels* today that, notwithstanding that genre's genesis and wholesale residence in the written word, subscribe to a more oral latticework of norms. But you need not take my word for this alone. I'll allow you to judge for yourselves based on a comparative textual analysis that cultural critic Anthony Easthope did of two works of fiction, Edward Rice Burroughs' *Tarzan of the Apes* and Joseph Conrad's novella *Heart of Darkness*.[10] These narratives could not rightly be differentiated on ideological grounds, Easthope argued, given that they equally reflected racist values and were just as uniformly driven by imperialist impulses and a masculinist point of view. So, where and in what did the variance lie? That, he deduced, was due to their very different modes of discourse. The methodological key thereby lay not in approaching the texts on the basis of what they meant, but from the vantage point of poetics, of each one's distinct literary or linguistic techniques.

Take a look at the properties of *Tarzan* that Easthope deemed fundamental to its type of storytelling—and which led to his concluding that its appeal to readers has to do with its functioning on the basis of the Freudian pleasure principle. That is, instinctively driven to experience pleasure and evade pain, readers are attracted to *Tarzan* because it is—

Concrete
Simple
Denotative (i.e., clear, as opposed to only implied or
oblique, signification)
Literal
Grounded in meaning that is immediate
Explicit
Univocal
Based in physical action
Visual (iconic)—and, guess what—
Unironic![11]

He also mentions the "overt" and "repetitious" nature of *Tarzan of the Ape's* racist ideology—which purportedly allows the reader to apprehend the novel in "a single reading."[12] Of course, as earlier I suggested, reticulate oral characteristics of narrative may feel more natural because they don't impose onto storytelling the sorts of interpretive moves that alphabetic literacy fosters—moves, incidentally, that those who cherish such literacy may fetishize.

As for what those latter literacy-inflected moves are: They can, in part, be discerned on the basis of the properties that Easthope teases out of *Heart of* Darkness. These include its "plurality of meaning," which makes the novella more complex, he says, because it demands more than a single reading. In fact, is rife with layers of meanings that are social, psychological, philosophical— "And so on and so on," Easthope declares.[13] Now, *Heart of Darkness* is one of my favorite works of literature, and I love to teach it, so please don't think I'm being *anti*-literate inflection here. But there's good reason for why this plurality of meaning might be absent from texts that function on the basis of a more oral sensibility. Like irony, a plurality of meaning endangers knowledge's safe communication, either by confusing or obscuring information. You can really only afford to say one thing at a time—or two at the most, in the case of punning. And the same goes for the listener taking in the story. Since a line of a story exists only in the moment of its utterance and then is immediately gone— forever—there's no time or space to unpack the just-uttered for possible additional, buried, or alternative significations. After all, we've already moved on—and on again.

But let's not be too hard on these former historians and critics. Or, rather, let's be forgiving, given that we *all* exist in paradigms of cultural making, and sometimes relatively unsuspectingly through no fault of our own. Moreover, we—especially those of us who study literature, critique it, write it—have become so far removed from an oral way of knowing that we may not be able to fathom the "genetic" makeup of a narrative contoured by orality as operating as anything other than for the solicitation of pleasure. (There's an unsettling paradox in Sigmund Freud having used the term "oral" to denote the first stage of his five-stage theory of psychosexual development—as representative of gratification by way of the mouth.) Indeed, we may need to be more sensitive when it comes to theorizing any convergence of literary criticism and psychoanalysis. I'd hardly dispute a connection between the dynamics of literature and the psyche, given that "to an important degree we define and construct our sense of self through our fictions …."[14] But when critics want to distinguish sophisticated reads and readerships—often by homing in on that plenitude of meaning that Easthope correctly detects in *Heart of Darkness*—their call on psychoanalysis to explain away the gratifyingly "univocal" fictions inadvertently belittles less inscriptively prepared readers.

In the case of psychoanalytic film theory, for instance, popular film is often read as pivoting on seductive screen figures that promote a spectator's slippage into a star's image, or as capitalizing on a spectator's desire; and because that desire is bound up with looking, it is said to induce narcissism, fetishism, and voyeurism. (Christian Metz called these "perceptual passions."[15]) But could these—indeed, could psychoanalytic theory more broadly be—a decidedly alphabetically literate way of reading a text that may have been circumscribed by orality? Consider, after all, the mnemonic force of a star's image. In fact, why should a spectator's ability to slip into that image be any more narcissistic or fetishistic than another spectator's privileging of screen subjectivity, or of the private decoding bound up with the presentation of a noncollective "I"?

The truth is, as human collectives, we are forever being made and remade by the very inventions we create: wheels, guns, the hearth, the plow, the assembly line, birth control, air conditioning, the compass, the computer, and, of course, that tiniest of big technologies, the alphabet. Derrick de Kerckhove even argues that the purpose of human psychology, both as a science and a fact of life, is "to provide a comprehensive and self-updating interpretation of our lives as they are being affected by our ever-changing cultural ground." Any baseline universality when it comes to humanity is merely a myth produced by "an eighteenth-century philosopher's wishful thinking."[16] That's why de Kerckhove coined the term *techno psychology*, akin to the accepted scientific term *biotechnology*. Our psychology is highly interanimated with our technologies, in other words: shaped by them, married to them—something that is also apparently in our nature (or psyche) to forget!

So, back to the historians and critics who are forwarding the intellectual agenda and, so, determining what gets studied, how it gets studied, and what gets said. Part of the larger problem when it comes to scholars, argues Yuval Noah Harari in *Sapiens: A Brief History of Humankind*, is that they tend "to ask only those questions that they can reasonably expect to answer." Yet, as Harari urges only a few sentences later—here explicitly with respect to the "curtain of silence" that paleontologically surrounds ancient humankind—"it is vital to ask questions for which no answers are available, otherwise we might be tempted to dismiss 60,000 of 70,000 years of human history with the excuse that 'the people who lived back then did nothing of importance.'"[17] As I mentioned early on in this book, by only beginning with or privileging "history"—by which I mean when human life and experience were finally recorded via some sort of external storage unit—we dismiss or, at least, diminish the significance of the tens of thousands of years of humankind as a fundamentally oral storytelling culture. In doing so, we may also be prone to overlooking the tenacity of some of the traits associated with orality that continued—and continue still—to persevere in alphabetically literate cultures. By cutting off contemporary, often mainstream culture from the prelit, we may also dangerously and unsympathetically dismiss *why* some stories are told in simple, concrete, denotative, Manichean, kinesthetically arousing, unironic ways. The prelit, you see, is still very much alive in the culture of lit.

Notes

1 Levine, *Highbrow/Lowbrow*, 5.
2 Bourdieu, *Distinction*.
3 Scholes and Kellogg, *Nature of Narrative*, 57.
4 I'm thankful to two educational websites for this information, Annenberg Learner and Khan Academy.
5 Graff, *Literacy Myths, Legacies*, 7.
6 Ibid.
7 Bordwell, *Planet Hong Kong*, 2.
8 Ibid., 2–20.
9 Levine, *Highbrow/Lowbrow*, 30–31.
10 Easthope, *Literary into Cultural Studies*. See particularly his chapter "High Culture/Popular Culture: *Heart of Darkness* and *Tarzan of the Apes*," 73–104.
11 Ibid., 87.
12 Ibid., 82.
13 Ibid.
14 Brooks, *Reading for the Plot*, 9.
15 Metz, *Imaginary Signifier*, 58.
16 De Kerckhove, *Skin of Culture*, 4.
17 Harari, *Sapiens*, 61.

References

Bordwell, David. *Planet Hong Kong: Popular Cinema and the Art of Entertainment*. Cambridge, MA: Harvard University Press, 2000.

Bourdieu, Pierre. *Distinction: A Social Critique of the Judgment of Taste*. Trans. Richard Nice. London: Routledge, 2010.

Brooks, Peter. *Reading for the Plot: Design and Intention in Narrative*. Cambridge, MA: Harvard University Press, 1992.

De Kerckhove, Derrick. *The Skin of Culture: Investigating the New Electronic Reality*. Ed. Christopher Dewdney. London: Kogan Page, 1997.

Easthope, Anthony. *Literary into Cultural Studies*. London: Routledge, 1991.

Graff, Harvey J. *Literacy Myths, Legacies, & Lessons: New Studies on Literacy.* New Brunswick, NJ: Transaction Publishers, 2011.

Harari, Yuval Noah. *Sapiens: A Brief History of Humankind.* New York: Random House, 2015.

Levine, Lawrence W. *Highbrow/Lowbrow: The Emergence of Cultural Hierarchy in America.* Cambridge, MA: Harvard University Press, 1988.

Metz, Christian. *The Imaginary Signifier: Psychoanalysis and the Cinema.* Trans. Celia Britton, Annwyl Williams, Ben Brewster, and Alfred Guzzetti. Bloomington: Indiana University Press, 1982.

Scholes, Robert, and Robert Kellogg. *The Nature of Narrative.* Oxford: Oxford University Press, 1968.

34 Why the humanities matter—to *all* of us

I want in this last chapter to set the stage for the next chapter—that is, for the sequel to this book, which, as you know by now, is titled *After Literature*. I'm not proclaiming this for marketing purposes, however much that might appear to be the case. Rather, it's because *Before Literature* is only half the story. It's the *pre*literacy story, accounting for what narrative was and had (and still has) to be when the epistemic and psychodynamic forces bound up with the written word have not yet intruded. It's also a story that I don't think has gotten sufficiently told, despite the clarity that it brings to the world *of* literature.

The great irony is, of course, that narrative molded out of an oral way of knowing could hardly have been excavated or even technically understood were it not for inscription. Thanks only to the distance literacy provides us, to the detachment writing permits us from what we know, are we able to undertake deeper and deeper levels of inspection, analysis, and interpretation, and with ever-expanding detail and accumulation, to boot. Is it any wonder, then, that, as Robert Scholes and Robert Kellogg declare with respect to Western literature (I cited a portion of this quote in the last chapter), "Homer is at once the culmination of oral narrative art and the inauguration of written."[1] Once the Iliad and Odyssey could be written down, everything about narrative art inclined toward change—and in some cases had no recourse *but* to change.

So, while what I've set out here comprises a complete, whole, and autonomous work, one dedicated to the constituents of that oral narrative art, it can, and perhaps even must, also operate as a metaphorical bookend: the *Before* as forerunner of the inscriptive *After*. In saying this, I'm by no means implying that the prelit is lesser than, inferior, or second-rate in comparison to the lit. (In philosophical parlance, that would entail a *teleology*, the expectation and belief that we are heading toward some unidirectional higher goal.) Rather, it's that I firmly believe we can only understand what literature *is*—not to mention, why it is the way it is, where it went, and how it got that way—if we see what storytelling could (and can) never be in an oral environment.

As for why I refer to *Before Literature* somewhat paradoxically as a bookend: The oral episteme of narrative as outlined here constitutes a paradigmatic extreme, a boundary-line, a limit—and also, unavoidably, a simplification. It's the only way, really, to meaningfully grasp and intellectually absorb this complex, fluid territory of storytelling—which is, of course, always enmeshed with (the equally complex, fluid nature of) distinctive cultures. But it's a worthwhile bookend, as far as I'm concerned. Of course, what being a bookend also figuratively implies is that this oral episteme is *not* a book. That is, rarely will any individual oral epic, or 1980s masala movie, or fairy tale ever satisfy all the characteristics elaborated in these pages. This prelit booken comprises instead a taxonomy, a general classification born of a prudent quarrying of commonalities from a broad array of oral epics, and masala movies, and fairy tales.

I've tried, at least, to complicate that boundary-line, to prevent a homogenizing of all orally inflected narrative by attending to some of the differences that have existed among cultures and storytelling forms through time. Often, I've done this via the illustrations in this book and the glosses that accompany them—foregrounding, for example, diverse mnemonic devices, or historical trajectories, or subgenres that have emerged in distinct environments. Still, I don't think it would be overreach to claim that we are at heart *Homo techne*, a species that has dominated (and not always nicely) because of our skills and aptitude for interanimating with technologies within our greater ecology. Nevertheless, individual cultures and groups have always done so in disparate ways—even when beholden to oral modes of storytelling. (Here, I'm thinking particularly of the distinctions between those painted cloths used in Rajasthan to facilitate recall of a narrative and that precious hand-held memory board from the Congo.)

No matter the extent to which we respect these traditional methods associated with orality, however, we should never forget that the world, generally speaking, has gone another route. Today, especially in our globalized landscape, those social developments that we identify with "civilization," "cultural evolution," and (some-times inaccurately) "progress" are almost exclusively imbricated with literacy. True, as that Malian griot Mamadou Kouyaté so wisely put it, "the future springs from the past"; but what the past means differs markedly when you no longer need to preserve it in your stories, when you can put it aside to mull instead (and quite wildly) on what the future might hold. In fact, we might even argue, in a bit of a Darwinian move, that literacy permitted story-telling not only to evolve but increasingly to *diverge*.[2]

Yet, when it comes to the discipline of literature and to the humanities more broadly, that future doesn't exactly look bright— at least not based on events of the last few decades. Enter into Google's search engine phrases like "Crisis of the Humanities" or "Threat to the Humanities" and you will find, as literary scholar and social activist for reading Philip Davis did, "23 million results, in a great fifty-year-long cry of distress, outrage, fear, and mel-ancholy."[3] Is this because—and here I'm speaking to my own immediate context in the United States—the humanities has become inconsequential in a world evermore wedded to STEM (Science, Technology, Engineering, Mathematics)? Or, more cyn-ically perhaps, is it, that there's no real money to be made from the study of literature, while both corporations and students can benefit from STEM? Alternatively, could we blame our culture for having slipped slowly into an anti-intellectualism that rejects sophisticated thought, rigorous analysis, and complex ideas? Or, perhaps less cynically this time, has the intellectual world slid too far into a narrow-mindedness of its own, with even the most progressive ideas too often lodged now in jargon and not STEM, not the humanities, not even Google impenetrable for most?

Perhaps we need to step back from these questions and this social maelstrom to remind ourselves that none of it—not STEM, not the humanities, not even Google—would have ever existed were it not for the invention of that most transformative of technologies, the written word. Maryanne Wolf, a language researcher known foremost for *Proust and the Squid: The Story and Science of the Reading Brain*, has called literacy "one of the most powerful cultural inventions that the species ever created." But as she also advises—especially in this, our digital age—we shouldn't lose sight of the "almost 200 million children and 600 million adults [who] will never attain anything approaching true literacy," calling that "waste of human potential … incalculable."[4]

The world in its current industrialized, globalized state has already gone literate—and if you don't join in or are denied that privilege, you lose out. Yet, at the same time, some literary texts may demand such a high level of literacy that even active readers find their meaning inscrutable, such that those readers turn against the humanities, accusing it of elitism and of fostering a form of navel-gazing that doesn't compute in a world of marketplace metrics. But remember when at the beginning of this book you, in the guise of that metaphoric fish, were pulled out of the water—your literate environment—in order to be made conscious of orality's sway on the composition, performance, and transmission of narrative? Well, in *After Literature,* you will get to inspect that water from above—which is to say, in a manner that will galvanize your understanding of the hows and whys of literature, "high literature" especially. We will inspect that water's various currents, streams, and even riptides (in the sense of what we may have lost while simultaneously making gains); and reflect on how much of *how* we think in and through literature was born precisely of our immersion in that water.

Ultimately, what *After Literature* will explicate for you is how the history and culture of literary narrative reflects the shifting course and current limits of our *epistemic DNA.*

Stay tuned.

Notes

1 Scholes and Kellogg, *Nature of Narrative*, 57.
2 This I borrow from Franco Moretti, who rhetorically queries, "And if language evolves by diverging, why not literature too?" (*Graphs, Maps, Trees*, 70).
3 Davis, "Series Introduction," v.
4 Wolf, *Tales of Literacy*, 1.

References

Davis, Philip. "Series Introduction." *Tales of Literacy for the 21st Century*, by Maryanne Wolf, with Stephanie Gottwald. Oxford: Oxford University Press, 2016. v–vi.

Moretti, Franco. *Graphs, Maps, Trees: Abstract Models for Literary History*. London: Verso Books, 2007.

Scholes, Robert, and Robert Kellogg. *The Nature of Narrative*. Oxford: Oxford University Press, 1968.

Wolf, Maryanne, with Stephanie Gottwald. *Tales of Literacy for the 21st Century*, by Maryanne Wolf. Oxford: Oxford University Press, 2016.

Index

Printed in the United States
by Baker & Taylor Publisher Services